GCSE OCR 21st Century Additional Applied Science

The Workbook

This book is for anyone doing **GCSE OCR 21st Century Additional Applied Science** at foundation level.

GCSE Science is all about **understanding how science works**. And not only that — understanding it well enough to be able to **question** what you hear on TV and read in the papers.

But you can't do that without a fair chunk of **background knowledge**. Hmm, tricky.

This book is full of **tricky questions**... each one designed to make you sweat — because that's the only way you'll get any **better**.

There are questions to see **what facts** you know. There are questions to see how well you can **apply those facts**. And there are questions to see how well you understand the role of **scientists** in the **real world**.

It's also got some daft bits in to try and make the whole experience at least vaguely entertaining for you.

What CGP is all about

Our sole aim here at CGP is to produce the highest quality books — carefully written, immaculately presented and dangerously close to being funny.

Then we work our socks off to get them out to you — at the cheapest possible prices.

Contents

MODULE 1 — LIFE CARE

Organisations Involved in Life Care 1
People Involved in Life Care 2
Medical History 3
Basic Tests 4
Extra Tests 6
Interpreting Test Results 8
Treatment 11
Prioritising Treatment and Resources 14
Health and Fitness Practitioners 15
The Blood and Blood Vessels 16
The Heart 17
The Breathing System 18
The Skeletal System 19
Pregnancy 20
Controlling Body Temperature 21
The Kidneys 22
Mixed Questions for Module 1 24

MODULE 2 — AGRICULTURE AND FOOD

Products from Organisms 27
Agriculture in the UK 28
Regulating Agriculture and Food 30
Products from Plants 31
The Plant Life-Cycle 32
Plant Growth 33
Crop Yield 35
Growing Plants 37
Cuttings and Tissue Culture 38
Products from Animals 39
Intensive and Organic Farming 40
Sexual Reproduction in Animals 41
Selective Breeding and Embryo Transplants 43
Products from Microorganisms 44
Growth of Microorganisms 47
Testing Food 48
The Food Market 50
Sustainable Agriculture 51
Mixed Questions for Module 2 53

MODULE 3 — SCIENTIFIC DETECTION

The Work of Scientific Detectives 56
Good Laboratory Practice 57
Visual Examination 58
Light Microscopes 60
Electron Microscopes 63
Chromatography 65
Electrophoresis 67
Colour Matching 68
Colorimetry 70
Scientific Evidence 71
Mixed Questions for Module 3 73

Module 4 — Harnessing Chemicals

Chemistry and Symbols	75
Laboratory Equipment	77
Acids and Alkalis	79
Reactions of Acids	81
Solutions	82
Making Insoluble Salts	84
Making Soluble Salts	86
Titrations	88
Organic and Inorganic Chemicals	89
Making Esters	91
Mixtures	92
Rates of Reaction	94
Sustainable Chemical Production	97
Chemical Purity	99
Industrial Production of Chemicals	100
Scaling Up	101
Planning Chemical Synthesis	102
Testing Formulations	104
Regulating the Chemical Industry	105
Mixed Questions for Module 4	106

Module 5 — Communications

Communicating Information	109
The Communications Industry	110
Designing Communication Systems	111
Jobs in the Communication Industry	113
Health and Safety	114
Flowcharts and Datasheets	116
Block Diagrams	118
Circuit Diagrams	121
Series and Parallel Circuits	123
Electric Current and Power	125
Wireless Communication	126
Analogue and Digital Signals	130
Converting Analogue to Digital	131
Communication Links	133
Pictures and Video	134
Mixed Questions for Module 5	135

Module 6 — Materials and Performance

Selecting Materials	138
Health and Safety	139
Mechanical Properties	140
Measuring Properties	142
Interpreting Data	144
Elastic and Plastic Behaviour	145
Metals, Ceramics and Polymers	147
Alloys and Composites	148
Materials and Forces	149
Electrical and Thermal Properties	151
Acoustic Properties	153
Optical Properties	156
Lenses	157
Lenses and Images	158
Camera Lenses	160
Matching Properties and Uses	161
Mixed Questions for Module 6	162

Published by Coordination Group Publications Ltd.

Editors:
Amy Boutal, Ellen Bowness, Tom Cain, Katherine Craig, Sarah Hilton,
Andy Park, Rose Parkin, Laurence Stamford, Jane Towle, Sarah Williams.

Contributors:
Mark A. Edwards, James Foster, Dr Iona M.J. Hamilton, Derek Harvey, Rebecca Harvey,
Andy Rankin, Philip Rushworth, Adrian Schmit, Claire Stebbing, Sophie Watkins.

ISBN: 978 1 84146 772 6

*With thanks to Jeremy Cooper, Barrie Crowther, Ian Francis, Sue Hocking, Glenn Rogers
and Julie Wakeling for the proofreading.*
With thanks to Laura Phillips for the copyright research.

*With thanks to the Department of the Environment, Food and Rural Affairs for permission to
reproduce the egg market data on page 28 (reproduced under the terms of the Click-Use Licence).*

With thanks to Nicholas Anderson for permission to use the photographs on page 59.

*With thanks to Science Photo Library for permission to reproduce the photograph used
on page 64.*

*With thanks to BSI for permission to reproduce the Kitemark symbol on page 115.
Kitemark and the Kitemark symbol are registered trademarks of BSI.*

Groovy website: www.cgpbooks.co.uk

Printed by Elanders Hindson Ltd, Newcastle upon Tyne.
Jolly bits of clipart from CorelDRAW®

Text, design, layout and original illustrations © Coordination Group Publications Ltd. 2007
All rights reserved.

Module 1 — Life Care

Organisations Involved in Life Care

Q1 After spending the summer eating pies, Richard has decided to **get fit**.

   a) Suggest a local indoor facility he could visit to improve his fitness.

      ....

   b) Which of the following would you expect to find at a fitness facility? Circle the correct answer(s).

      weights   X-ray machines   treadmills   doctors   aerobics classes

Q2 An elderly woman has fallen down some stairs. Her neighbour phones for an **ambulance** to take her to the **local hospital**. Suggest one place, other than a hospital, where she could go to be checked.

....

Q3 A teacher at a local school has asked a **nurse** to come and talk to the pupils about the **National Health Service**.

   a) Fill in the passage below using words from the list.

specialist care	hospitals	dentistry	some	gyms	all

The National Health Service (NHS) owns and runs the majority of the UK's .... It also provides many other health care services, such as .... The NHS makes sure that health care is available to .... citizens and that .... is provided, even if it's not available locally.

   b) Apart from providing diagnoses and treatment, describe one other function of the NHS.

....

Q4 Aisha is a **manager** in the **NHS**. Most of her time is spent deciding how to **allocate resources** in the best possible way.

Important Resources:
- Choc. Biscuits
- Cake...

Which of the following are resources that Aisha will have to allocate? Circle the **three** correct answers.

money for buildings   patients   illnesses   equipment   staff

People Involved in Life Care

Q1 Dr Walker is a **general practitioner** (GP).

a) Describe the role of a GP.

....

....

....

b) If one of his patients is having long-term treatment, Dr Walker arranges regular appointments with them. Underline the reasons why this is a good idea.

It is good exercise for the patient to go to the doctor's surgery.

It can help strengthen the relationship between doctor and patient.

It increases the income of the NHS.

It allows the doctor to check whether the patient is improving.

c) In Dr Walker's waiting room there are several leaflets published by organisations like the Department of Health and the British Lung Foundation.

i) Why is it important to educate the public about health issues?

....

....

ii) Suggest one way, other than by publishing leaflets, of educating people about health issues.

....

Top Tips: Lots of people are involved in life care — GPs, nurses, paramedics, midwives, fitness trainers... you need to describe the role of at least two of them, including a decent job description.

Module 1 — Life Care

Medical History

Q1 Ann has recently moved to a new town and needs to **register** with a **doctor**. When she goes to the surgery she is given a form full of **questions** to answer.

  a) One question asks if there is a history of cancer or diabetes in her family. Which of these statements correctly explains why her doctor would want this information? Tick any that apply.

  ☐ So the doctor can register her family members as well.

  ☐ So the doctor knows whether Ann is more likely to get either disease.

  ☐ Ann won't be allowed to register with the new doctor if members of her family have had either disease.

  b) Why might the questionnaire ask if she is taking any long-term medication?

  ....

  ....

  c) What other things might Ann be asked about? Underline the **three** correct answers.

  how much TV she watches   how much exercise she does

  whether she's had any previous illnesses   how much alcohol she drinks

  her annual income

Q2 David consults a **fitness trainer** at his gym to get some advice on an exercise programme.

  a) The trainer asks David whether he has ever had problems with any of his joints. Suggest why the trainer would want to know this.

  ....

  b) David is **diabetic**. He regularly takes insulin to control his blood sugar levels. Is it important that his fitness trainer knows this? Explain your answer.

  ....

  ....

Module 1 — Life Care

Basic Tests

Q1 Jeremy wants to become a **pilot** in the RAF. Before he is interviewed he has to pass a **health assessment**.

a) During the assessment, a doctor measures Jeremy's pulse rate. Tick the boxes to show whether these statements about taking someone's pulse rate are **true** or **false**.

                                                                            True   False

    i) Pulse rates are measured using a thermometer.

    ii) You need a stopwatch or a watch with a second hand to take an accurate pulse rate.

    iii) Pulse rate is usually measured at an artery in the shoulder.

b) Next, the doctor wants to calculate Jeremy's **BMI**.

    i) What does BMI stand for?

    ....

    ii) What information does he need? Circle the **two** correct answers.

        Jeremy's percentage body fat   Jeremy's body mass   Jeremy's age   Jeremy's height

c) What equipment would the doctor use to measure Jeremy's body mass?

....

d) The doctor tells Jeremy that he is about to use a piece of equipment called a sphygmomanometer. What does a sphygmomanometer measure?

....

e) At the end of the health assessment the doctor measures Jeremy's **aerobic fitness**. Which of the following tests can be used to assess aerobic fitness? Tick any correct boxes.

    step test ☐

    electrocardiograph ☐

    blood test ☐

    bleep test ☐

Jeremy's fitness was terrible, but he had a cool hat.

Module 1 — Life Care

Basic Tests

Q2 A **paramedic** is attending to a man who is feeling dizzy.

a) The paramedic checks his **pulse rate**. He counts 33 pulses in 30 seconds. What is the man's pulse rate?

....

b) The paramedic suspects that the man is suffering from heat stroke. Give three types of thermometer that the paramedic could use to check the man's body temperature.

1. ....

2. ....

3. ....

Q3 **Fitness instructors** need to know certain information about a person before they can design a **fitness programme** for them.

a) Suggest **two** pieces of basic information that a fitness instructor might need.

....

....

b) Why is it important for a fitness instructor to keep an accurate record of any information they collect about a person? Underline any correct statements.

So that the fitness instructor can check their progress.

So that other members of the fitness team can use the information to help the person.

So that the government can keep records of how healthy everyone is.

Because gyms often put their members' information on their website.

Top Tips: These two pages might be called 'Basic Tests', but don't make the mistake of thinking your exam will be basic — those pesky examiners really like to test you. If you really want to impress, learn to spell that sphygo.. sphygomoma-wotsit... you know the one I mean.

Module 1 — Life Care

Extra Tests

Q1 Amina is a **radiographer** at a private clinic. She is asked to give a talk on the use of **X-rays** in medicine.

Circle the correct word(s) in each pair to complete her introduction.

> X-ray imaging is a(n) **invasive / non-invasive** technique, which means that it involves **some / no** surgery. X-rays are normally used in medicine to examine **bones / organs**. The rays pass straight through **tissue / bone** but are absorbed by **tissue / bone**, which means they can provide information about the **structures / functions** in the body.

Q2 Karen is in hospital. She is being monitored by an **electrocardiograph**. The graph produced by this machine is shown below.

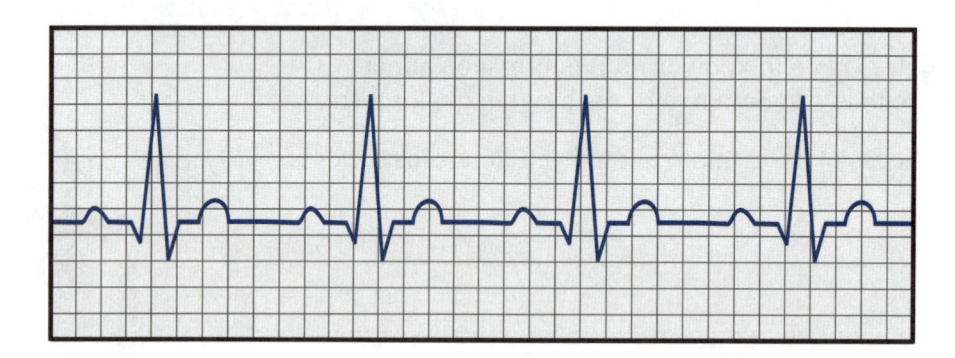

a) What is an electrocardiograph used to monitor?

....

b) What is the name given to the graph created by an electrocardiograph?

....

c) How does an electrocardiograph work? Underline the correct answer.

It measures temperature changes.   *It measures sound waves.*

It measures electrical activity.

d) The hospital staff need to perform some tests on Karen's blood. Describe how a nurse would take a **blood sample** from Karen.

....

....

Module 1 — Life Care

Extra Tests

Q3 A doctor suspects his patient may have cystitis — an inflammation of the bladder lining. The doctor asks for a **urine sample** to help his diagnosis.

a) i) Which of the following substances is a urine sample normally tested for? Circle the correct answer.

water   urea   protein   calcium

ii) Cystitis can be caused by a **bacterial infection**.
What will be present in the sample if the patient has a bacterial infection?
....

b) **Test sticks** can be used to analyse the sample. Complete the following sentences about test sticks by circling the correct word(s).

> Test sticks are commonly used in surgeries to examine urine samples.
> They are **more** / **less** accurate than sending the sample to a laboratory,
> and take up **more** / **less** time. For this reason, if a test stick is positive it
> **needs** / **doesn't need** to be sent away for confirmation.

Q4 **Ultrasound scanning** can be used to make images of developing fetuses.

a) Why is it useful for doctors to be able to see a fetus in the womb?
....
....

b) Tick the boxes to show whether the following statements about ultrasound are **true** or **false**.

	True	False
i) Ultrasound is only used on pregnant women.	☐	☐
ii) Ultrasound is used to make images of a fetus because it is safer than X-rays.	☐	☐
iii) Ultrasound uses ultraviolet radiation to make images.	☐	☐

Top Tips: There are lots of tests you need to know about for this 'extra tests' section, but thankfully not in too much detail. Make sure you've got the basics covered for urine tests, blood tests, ECGs, ultrasound and X-rays. Now turn over to see if you know what the results mean...

Module 1 — Life Care

Interpreting Test Results

Q1 Tom is talking to his friend Steve about **pulse rates**.

  a) Tom thinks that the average adult pulse rate is about 55 beats per minute. Steve thinks it is closer to 75. Whose estimate is nearest to the correct value?

  ....

  b) Tom checks his pulse during a run and finds that his heart is beating about 130 times per minute. Why does your pulse rate need to increase during exercise?

  ....

  c) Give a reason, other than exercise, why someone's pulse rate might be high. Circle any correct answers.

  low blood pressure   heart disorders   cardiovascular shock   anxiety   panic attack

Q2 Katie has flu. She takes her **temperature**, which she finds to be 37.9 °C.

  a) Which statement best describes Katie's temperature? Tick the box next to the correct statement.

  ☐ Katie's temperature is too high.

  ☐ Katie's temperature is too low.

  ☐ It's impossible to know if Katie's temperature is too high or low because body temperature varies greatly.

  b) Katie's body temperature may be affected by her flu infection. What word describes an elevated body temperature due to an infection?

  ....

  c) Give one other reason why someone's body temperature might be:

  i) higher than average.

  ....

  ii) lower than average.

  ....

Module 1 — Life Care

Interpreting Test Results

Q3 Duncan has had his **blood pressure** measured. The reading was 134/92 mmHg.

a) Is Duncan's blood pressure normal?

....

b) Duncan's friend Mark has a poor diet and does very little exercise compared to Duncan. Would you expect his blood pressure to be higher or lower than Duncan's?

....

Q4 A young boy fell off his bicycle and landed on his right arm. He was in a lot of pain so he went to hospital for an **X-ray**.

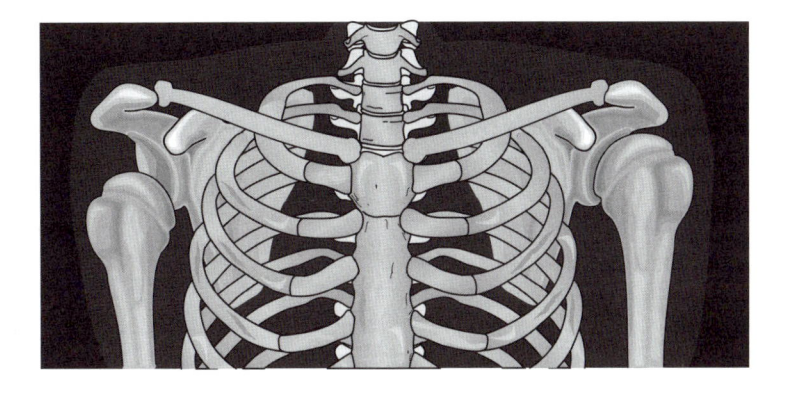

What injury has the X-ray identified?

....

Q5 The following passage is about making diagnoses from **blood samples**. Fill in the gaps using words from the list below.

| heart disease | anaemia | heat stroke | kidney disease | infection | liver disease |

Blood tests can help identify many disorders. For example, ... can be identified by looking at enzyme levels. Examining the number of red blood cells in the blood can help in diagnosing some types of ....

Module 1 — Life Care

Interpreting Test Results

Q6 Louise and Charlotte have their **body mass** measured when they join a gym. Louise has a mass of 54 kg and Charlotte has a mass of 73 kg.

a) Tick the box to show which statement is **true**.

☐ Louise is a normal weight but Charlotte is overweight.

☐ Louise is underweight but Charlotte is a normal weight.

☐ You cannot tell if Louise and Charlotte are overweight or underweight without more information.

b) Louise calculates her body mass index (BMI) as 17.7. Charlotte's is 26.7. Using the table on the right, what advice would be given to each of them if they wanted to be a healthy weight?

BMI	Condition
<18.5	underweight
18.5 - 24.9	healthy weight
25 - 29.9	overweight
>30	obese

Louise: ....

Charlotte: ....

c) Charlotte's friend Andrew has a BMI of 29.3. According to the BMI table he is nearly obese and needs to lose weight. However, he doesn't think that he's overweight. Could he be correct? Tick the correct box.

☐ Yes — having excess body fat is normally perfectly healthy.

☐ Yes — if he exercises regularly, his extra weight might be due to muscle rather than fat.

☐ No — if his BMI is too high then he should definitely lose weight.

Q7 **Glucose** was found in a **urine sample** from a patient.

a) Name the condition that could have caused this.

....

b) The patient had suspected that this would be the result of the test, but she is relieved that no blood was found in the sample. What would this have suggested? Circle the correct answer.

heart disease   liver disease   kidney damage

Top Tips: It's not much good remembering all these tests if you've no idea what the results mean, so make sure you can answer all the questions on the last three pages. It's not too bad really — most of it's just a case of learning what's normal then pointing out things that aren't.

Module 1 — Life Care

Treatment

Q1 Mick has damaged one of the **discs** in his back. His doctor tells him about the **possible treatments**, which are described below.

> Option 1: take painkillers to help the pain.
>
> Option 2: take gentle exercise, e.g. walking or swimming.
>
> Option 3: physiotherapy to ease pressure around the damaged disc.
>
> Option 4: an operation to repair the damaged disc.

a) Some of the options will treat Mick's symptoms, but won't cure the problem.
Give **one** option that would:

  i) only treat Mick's symptoms. ....

  ii) cure his damaged disc. ....

b) Suggest another situation when a doctor might prescribe a treatment that eases the patient's symptoms without curing them.

....

....

c) Mick is in a lot of pain, so his doctor prescribes the painkiller ibuprofen. Like many drugs, ibuprofen can cause side-effects.

Underline the reason why Mick's doctor has prescribed ibuprofen even though it could cause side-effects.

WARNING: may cause extreme hairstyles.

Side-effects only affect people who are already ill.

Without ibuprofen Mick's back will get worse.   **The benefits outweigh the risks of side-effects.**

d) Six weeks after Mick hurt his back it is still no better.
His doctor recommends an operation to mend Mick's disc.

  i) Suggest why Mick's doctor waited so long before advising an operation.

  ....

  ii) When Mick goes to hospital for the operation he is asked to sign an 'informed consent' form. Why does he need to do this?

  ....

  ....

Module 1 — Life Care

Treatment

Q2 Carla plays **hockey** for her local team. During a match she **hurts her leg**. The **physiotherapist** says that she has injured a **muscle**, and treats it straight away.

a) The physiotherapist treats Carla's injury using the steps below. Write them out in the correct order.

compression   elevation   rest   ice

....

b) After the swelling on her leg has gone down, Carla's physiotherapist shows her a series of exercises to work through during the next few weeks. Number the boxes below to put the exercises in the correct order.

☐ Gentle jogging to build up pre-injury levels of strength and muscle usage.

☐ Return to hockey training, gradually building up intensity.

☐ Stretching and weight-bearing exercises to improve the strength of the injured muscle.

☐ Gentle exercise such as walking and swimming to regain movement and maintain aerobic fitness.

☐ Simple stretching exercises to regain flexibility in the muscle.

Q3 Stuart wants to join the police force but doesn't think he's **fit** enough. His doctor recommends that he goes to see a **fitness instructor** and a **nutritionist**.

a) Stuart wants to improve his general fitness, rather than focusing on a specific part of his body. Suggest **two** pieces of advice that the fitness instructor might give Stuart.

....

....

b) The nutritionist advises Stuart to eat a healthy, balanced diet. Suggest **two** features of such a diet.

....

....

Q4 Dolby City Hospital employs several **surgeons**.

Describe one operation that surgeons might carry out to improve a patient's health.

....

....

Module 1 — Life Care

Treatment

Q5 Dwayne is the best **cross-country runner** in his school. He is currently training for the **county championships** and is working on improving his **aerobic fitness**.

Dwayne measures his aerobic fitness using the Harvard Step Test, which is described below.

1) Carry out step-up for 5 minutes.
2) Rest for 1 minute.
3) Measure your pulse rate.
4) Calculate a 'fitness score' from the pulse rate.

a) Dwayne measures his fitness every two weeks and writes the results in his training diary. Suggest **one** reason why Dwayne records his fitness score every time he does the test.

....

b) Dwayne wants to make sure that his results are both accurate and reliable. Tick the boxes to show whether the actions below help make his data accurate, reliable or both.

Accurate   Reliable

i) Using a stopwatch to time each part of the test. ☐ ☐

ii) Using the same height step every time he performs the test. ☐ ☐

iii) Carrying out the same number of step-ups every time he does the test. ☐ ☐

c) Six weeks before the championships, Dwayne changed the exercises in his fitness programme. Suggest **two** reasons why he might have done this.

....

....

Q6 An elderly woman needs an **operation** to replace a damaged **valve** in her heart. But, because she is very **overweight**, her doctor has said she needs to **lose weight** before the operation.

a) Describe how the woman could monitor her progress **during** a weight-loss programme.

....

b) The doctor continues to monitor the woman's health **after** the operation. Explain why.

....

....

Top Tips: After a health or fitness practitioner devises a programme for a patient or client, they don't just put their feet up and leave them to get on with it. Instead they keep meeting up for a good gossip... err sorry, to check the person's progress and make sure the plan is working nicely.

Module 1 — Life Care

Prioritising Treatment and Resources

Q1 Heather is waiting in the **accident and emergency department** of a hospital with a suspected **broken arm**. She is frustrated because some people who arrived after her are being **treated before** her.

The table below shows the people needing treatment.

Name	Age	Condition
Heather	27	Suspected broken arm
Joe	5	Having an asthma attack, cannot breathe
Mary	83	Suspected broken arm
Philip	34	Major blood loss from deep cut on leg
Kate	26	Head injury, conscious but in a lot of pain

a) **i)** Who should be treated first? ....

ii) Give a reason for your answer.

....

b) Heather and Mary have similar injuries. Why is Mary treated before Heather?

....

c) Who would be treated last? ....

Q2 A new **health and fitness** centre has opened. Caroline's job is to **manage its facilities** to make sure that the centre makes a profit.

Tick the boxes to show whether the following statements are **true** or **false**.   True   False

a) Caroline has to make sure the amount of money the centre spends is less than the income from clients.   ☐ ☐

b) Staff wages are not an important part of Caroline's budget.   ☐ ☐

c) Caroline should spend money on the facilities that are popular and close or remove those that aren't being used.   ☐ ☐

Top Tips: Making somebody who's in pain wait for treatment might sound cruel, but if it means that somebody else's life can be saved in the meantime, it makes sense. Being a health practitioner isn't easy — you often have to make tough decisions based on the evidence available.

Module 1 — Life Care

Health and Fitness Practitioners

Q1 A **careers adviser** has asked a class of GCSE students to write lists of their **personal qualities**. She will use these to help the students decide what kind of career they might be **suited** to. Three of the students' lists are shown below.

A
1) good listener
2) patient
3) trustworthy
4) sensitive
5) understanding

B
1) hard-working
2) reliable
3) ambitious
4) competitive
5) blunt

C
1) imaginative
2) artistic
3) creative
4) thoughtful
5) original

a) Which student do you think is best suited to being a **health practitioner**? Circle the correct answer.

    A   B   C

b) The careers adviser arranges for the students to meet Michael, a nurse from the local hospital.

  i) Michael says it's important to develop a professional relationships with patients. Circle the words below that describe how a professional relationship should be.

    emotional   personal   prejudiced   detached   indifferent   dishonest

  ii) Michael describes a difficult situation he once faced. A patient had been given a special diet to help her lose weight. The patient said she had stuck to the diet but wasn't losing weight.

Tick the boxes by the statements describing what a health practitioner **should** do in this situation.

- Tell the patient off for not sticking to their diet. ☐
- Decide how to proceed based on what the patient says and the evidence. ☐
- Talk to the patient. Ask questions and listen carefully to her answers to try and understand why the diet is not working. ☐
- Offer the patient money to stick to their diet. ☐
- Consider whether the diet needs changing so that it fits in better with the patient's family or work life. ☐

  iii) The students find Michael very easy to talk to. Give **three** reasons why it is important for health practitioners to have good communication skills.

....

....

....

Module 1 — Life Care

The Blood and Blood Vessels

Q1 Pathologists can diagnose some diseases by studying blood samples.

a) Name three components of blood.

1. ....

2. ....

3. ....

b) Which type of blood cell transports oxygen?

....

Q2 The NHS has designed a leaflet explaining what causes varicose veins.

Complete the following paragraph from the leaflet, using words from the box.

| higher | forwards | valves | thicker | backwards | thinner | lower | from | to |

Varicose veins are swollen and irregularly shaped and may be painful. They are caused by weakened vein walls. Veins have .... walls than arteries because they transport blood at .... pressure. Veins transport blood .... the heart, often against the flow of gravity, so they have .... to stop the blood flowing the wrong way. However, if these are not working properly blood may flow ...., damaging the walls of the vein and causing varicose veins.

Q3 Huang has been taken to the accident and emergency department of the hospital. He fell off his bike and has a cut that won't stop bleeding. The doctor tells Huang he has injured an artery and needs an operation to stop the bleeding.

a) i) What is the function of arteries? ....

ii) Give **one** way that the structure of an artery is specialised for this function.

....

b) Huang also has bruises on his knees where capillaries have been broken. Capillaries break easily because they have very thin walls.

Why is it useful for capillaries to have such thin walls?

....

....

Module 1 — Life Care

The Heart

Q1 Padma has been told that she has a high risk of developing **heart disease**.

Her cardiologist explains that heart disease is caused by a build-up of fatty substances in the arteries that supply the heart. This restricts the blood flow to the heart and can cause damage.

a) **i)** Label the diagram of the heart below, using words from the box.

| right atrium | left ventricle | right ventricle | left atrium |

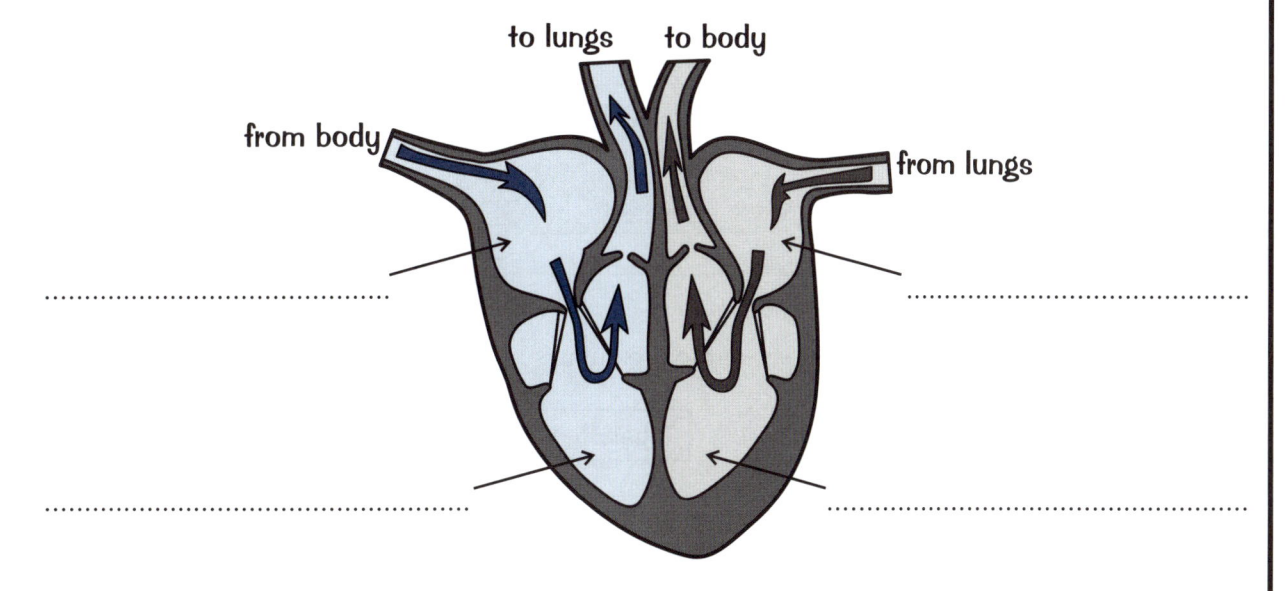

ii) Circle **two valves** on the diagram.

b) The statements below describe the flow of blood **from the body** through the heart and lungs. Number the boxes to put the statements in the correct order. The first one has been done for you.

☐ Blood passes into the left ventricle, which pumps it out and round the whole body.

☐ Blood flows through a valve into the right ventricle.

☐ Blood leaves the heart and flows to the lungs.

[1] Deoxygenated blood from the body enters the right atrium.

☐ Oxygenated blood from the lungs flows into the left atrium.

Module 1 — Life Care

The Breathing System

Q1 Paul has a persistent cough and often wheezes when he breathes. His **doctor** thinks that he may have a chest infection.

a) Label the diagram of the breathing system.

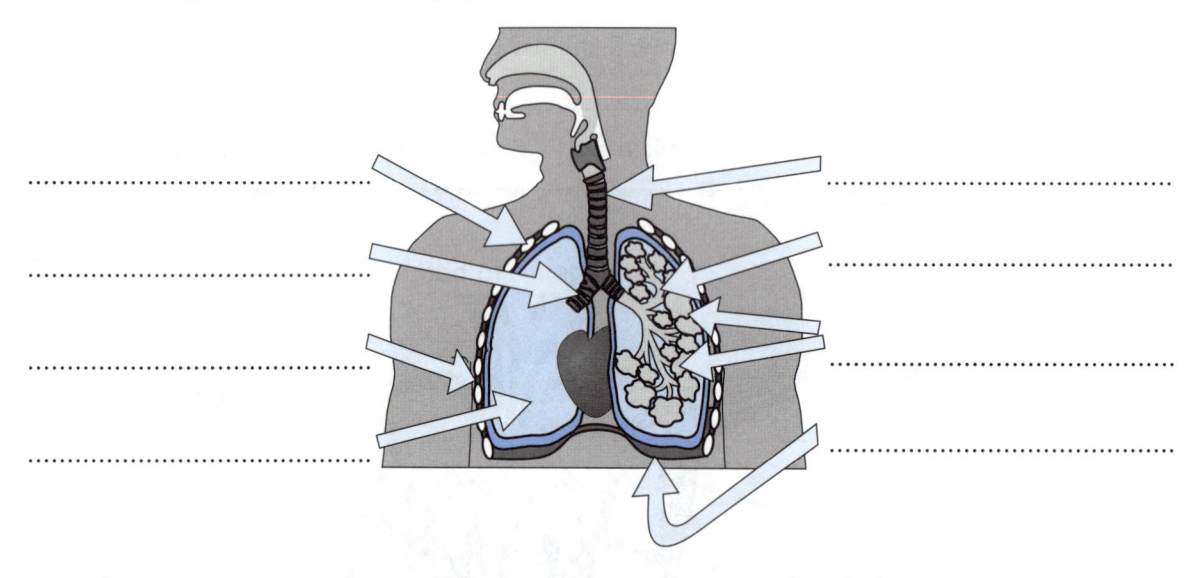

b) Draw lines to connect each part of the breathing system to its description.

- alveoli — Tubes that transport gases into and out of the lungs.
- bronchi — Tiny air sacs that provide a large surface area for gas exchange.
- diaphragm — Muscle below the lungs that contracts and relaxes to help with breathing.
- intercostal muscles — A set of muscles that raise and lower the ribs to help with breathing.
- lungs — Bones that protect the heart and lungs and help with breathing.
- ribs — Pipe that connects the mouth and nose to the lungs.
- trachea — Organs for the exchange of oxygen and carbon dioxide.

c) Circle the correct word(s) in each pair to complete the following sentences.

i) When Paul breathes in, his intercostal muscles and diaphragm **contract** / relax. This moves the ribcage **up and out** / down and in, which **increases** / decreases the volume of the lungs, causing air to enter.

ii) To breathe out, the muscles in Paul's chest contract / **relax**. This **increases** / decreases the pressure in his lungs, which forces air out.

Top Tips: Don't forget, air moves in and out of the lungs because the intercostal muscles and diaphragm contract and relax to change the pressure — air doesn't just move in and out on its own.

Module 1 — Life Care

The Skeletal System

Q1 **Radiologists** use X-rays to take images of the **skeletal system**.

a) Complete the table by writing each letter from the diagram in the correct box.

Letter	Bone
	clavicle
	femur
	fibula
	humerus
	pelvis
	radius
	ribs
	scapula
	skull
	sternum
	tibia
	ulna
	vertebral column

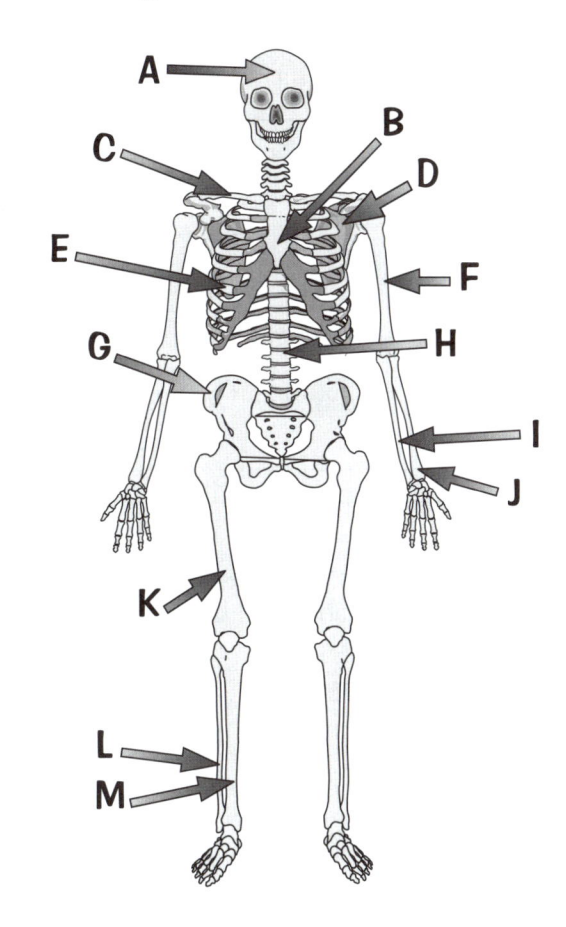

b) The skeleton has three functions — **support**, **movement** and **protection**. Which of the three functions correctly describes each example below?

   i) The skull covers the brain and is very tough. ....

   ii) The vertebral column helps to keep the body upright. ....

   iii) The biceps muscle is attached by tendons to the scapula and radius. ....

Q2 Caroline has hurt her leg playing **rounders**. A **physiotherapist** shows her a diagram of the **calf muscle** to help explain her injury.

Tick the boxes to show whether the following statements are **true** or **false**.

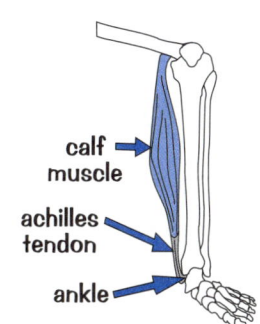

		True	False
a)	Caroline's calf muscle is attached to her bones by tendons.	☐	☐
b)	When a tendon contracts it moves the calf muscle.	☐	☐
c)	When the calf muscle contracts it pulls on the bone.	☐	☐
d)	The bones in Caroline's knee are held together by ligaments.	☐	☐
e)	Ligaments are very strong and quite elastic.	☐	☐

Module 1 — Life Care

Pregnancy

Q1 A school nurse has produced a hand-out to give to pupils in a **sex education** class.

Fill in the gaps in the paragraph from the hand-out using words from the box.
You may use each word once, more than once or not at all.

cervix   fallopian tube   28   vagina   fertilised   endometrium   uterus   ovaries
One of the two .... produces an egg every .... days. The egg passes into the .... where it may meet sperm that have entered through the .... during sexual intercourse. If the egg is .... by a sperm, it will attach itself to the .... (the lining of the ....) and begin to develop into a baby. If the egg is not fertilised, it travels through the .... then out through the .... during a period.

Q2 An antenatal class is being shown the diagrams below. These show the uterus **before** pregnancy and how it will change **during** pregnancy.

Before pregnancy — wall of uterus, endometrium, cervix

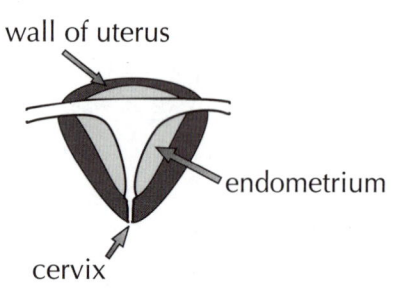

During pregnancy — wall of uterus, umbilical cord, amnion, developing baby (fetus), amniotic fluid, placenta, cervix

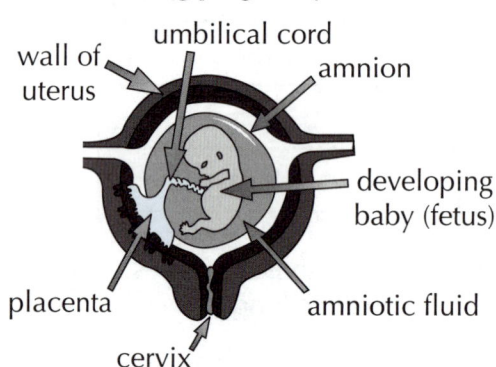

   a) Describe what happens to the uterus during pregnancy.

      ....

   b) What is the function of the following parts shown in the diagram?

      i) amnion ....

      ii) placenta ....

      iii) umbilical cord ....

   c) Describe what happens to each of the following parts during the birth of the baby.

      i) amnion ....

      ii) placenta ....

      iii) muscles in the uterus ....

Module 1 — Life Care

Controlling Body Temperature

Q1 Yolanda and Subarna are from England and are on holiday in **Egypt**, where the daytime **temperature** can be very **high**.

  a) Tick the boxes to show whether the statements are **true** or **false**.

  True False

  i) Yolanda's cheeks go red when she is hot because the blood flow in the capillaries close to the surface of her skin increases. ☐ ☐

  ii) More heat is lost to the surroundings when blood vessels close to the skin's surface are smaller in diameter. ☐ ☐

  iii) Yolanda and Subarna are likely to sweat more than usual. ☐ ☐

  iv) Sweating causes the body to retain heat. ☐ ☐

  v) The evaporation of sweat from the skin helps the body to lose heat. ☐ ☐

  b) How does the body identify a change in skin temperature?

  ....

  ....

Q2 A mountain rescue team found an injured climber who was suffering from hypothermia — a **dangerously low body temperature**.

  a) The climber's skin was very pale.
  Circle the correct word from each pair in the passage below to explain why.

  > Blood vessels close to the surface of his skin got smaller / larger in diameter. This meant that more / less blood flowed to the surface of his skin and it appeared pale. This stopped the blood from losing / gaining as much heat to / from the surroundings.

  b) **i)** Other than by changing blood flow, give one way that the climber's body would have tried to maintain his body temperature, to avoid hypothermia.

  ....

  ii) Explain how the response given in part i) helps to maintain body temperature.

  ....

Top Tips: When it comes to monitoring itself, your body is really quite impressive — you have a sort of built-in thermometer in your brain that constantly monitors your body temperature. If the temperature isn't quite right, all sorts of processes jump into action to bring it back to the norm.

Module 1 — Life Care

The Kidneys

Q1 **Sports scientists** studied the effect of **water intake** on **urine production**. Groups of people drank a set volume of water over **24 hours**, and the volume of **urine** they produced was recorded.

Their results are shown on the graph opposite.

a) What happened to the **volume of urine** produced as the volume of water drunk increased? Circle the correct answer.

　　it increased　　it stayed the same　　it decreased

b) How much water would you expect the group that produced the **palest** urine to have drunk? Circle the correct answer.

　　0.5 l　　1 l　　1.5 l　　2 l　　2.5 l　　3 l　　3.5 l

c) Which organ in the body produces urine? Circle the correct answer.

　　bladder　　kidney　　gall bladder　　sphincter　　liver

d) Give **two** ways, other than in urine, in which water is lost from the body.

　　...

Q2 One of the possible **side effects** of the medicine Milly is taking is **kidney damage**. She has regular **blood tests** to make sure her kidneys are working properly.

a) The tests measure the amount of **urea** in Milly's blood.

　i) What is urea? ....

　ii) Why is it important that it is removed from the blood?

　　...

b) The test also measures the concentration of **ions** in Milly's blood.

　i) Why is it dangerous to have a very high or a very low ion content in the body?

　　...

　　...

　ii) Give **two** ways in which ions are removed from the body.

　　...

c) Milly's doctor also tests her urine for **proteins**.
Why would the presence of protein in Milly's urine indicate that her kidneys might be damaged?

　　...

Module 1 — Life Care

The Kidneys

Q3 Omid has a **kidney stone**. A **urologist** draws Omid a diagram to show him where the stone is.

Use the words in the box below to complete the labels on this diagram of a **nephron**.

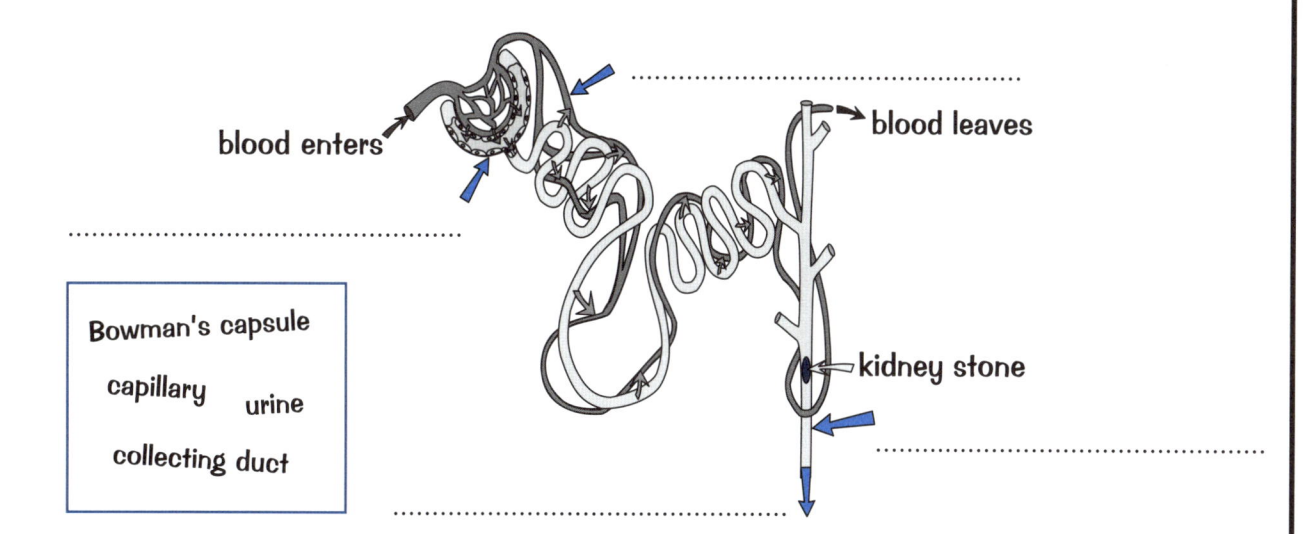

Bowman's capsule
capillary   urine
collecting duct

Q4 People who suffer from **kidney failure** may need **dialysis**. Dialysis machines **filter** blood in the same way that a healthy kidney would.

a) List the things that a healthy kidney:

i) filters out of the blood ....

ii) reabsorbs ....

iii) releases in urine ....

Billy the kid-ney bean

b) Complete the passage using words from the box, to describe how a healthy kidney works.

| nephron | ureter | reabsorbed | urine | Bowman's | bladder | capsule | membrane | high |

When blood enters the kidneys, a .... pressure is built up. This squeezes small

molecules out of the blood and into the ....

A .... acts as a filter, stopping large molecules moving out of the blood.

The filtered liquid flows along the .... The useful substances are

.... The remaining substances leave the nephron and flow through the

.... to the .... for removal from the body as ....

Top Tips: Kidneys do loads of important jobs — that's why is so dangerous if they go wrong. You can live with only one kidney though — so it's possible for some people with kidney failure to receive a donated kidney from a member of their family or from another suitable donor.

Module 1 — Life Care

Mixed Questions for Module 1

Q1 Rob was **rock scrambling** when he lost his footing and slipped into the lake below. His friend called the **emergency services**, who took Rob to **hospital**.

   a) Describe how the paramedic in the ambulance would measure the following. Include details of the equipment they would use.

   i) Rob's pulse rate ....

   ....

   ii) Rob's temperature ....

   ....

   b) The paramedic finds that Rob's pulse rate is 75 bpm, but is worried because the pulse is **weak**. Suggest why Rob's pulse is weak.

   ....

   c) Rob's temperature is 34 °C. What condition is Rob is suffering from?

   ....

   d) When Rob arrives at the hospital there are lots of people waiting to be treated. Number the boxes below to show the order in which these patients would be treated.

   ☐ A chef who has cut his finger while chopping vegetables.

   ☐ A child who is choking and cannot breathe.

   ☐ A lady who is bleeding from a head injury.

   e) Rob hurt his leg when he fell, so he has an X-ray. The result is shown below.

   i) What is the name of the bone that Rob has injured? ....

   ii) Describe what is wrong with it. ....

   f) At the hospital, Rob is treated by several different medical practitioners. Give the title and role of one type of practitioner who may have treated Rob.

   Title: .... Role: ....

   ....

Module 1 — Life Care

Mixed Questions for Module 1

Q2 Lucy has gone to see her **GP** because she is worried that her **lifestyle** is putting her at risk of **heart disease**.

a) i) Suggest **two** questions that Lucy's GP may ask her before he gives any advice.

....

....

ii) Why is it important that the GP records Lucy's answers?

....

b) Being overweight is a risk factor for heart disease. The GP measures Lucy's height and weight so he can determine her body mass index. Lucy is 1.58 m tall and weighs 83 kg.

$$BMI = \frac{body\ mass\ in\ kg}{(height\ in\ m)^2}$$

i) Calculate Lucy's BMI. ....

ii) Is Lucy overweight? Give a reason for your answer.

BMI	Condition
<18.5	underweight
18.5 - 24.9	healthy weight
25 - 29.9	overweight
>30	obese

....

....

c) The GP takes a sample of Lucy's blood. He sends it to the pathology lab to see if Lucy is at risk of developing heart disease.

Suggest how a blood test could indicate whether Lucy is at risk of developing heart disease.

....

Q3 Susie is **pregnant**. She has decided to employ a **private midwife** — this will ensure that she always sees the same person.

a) Give **one** advantage of regular contact between Susie and her midwife.

....

b) Susie interviewed a few people when choosing a midwife. Suggest **two** personal qualities that a good midwife should have.

....

c) The midwife explains the changes that will happen to Susie's body during her pregnancy. Describe **two** changes the midwife would have explained.

....

....

Module 1 — Life Care

Mixed Questions for Module 1

Q4 Tom suffers from **asthma**. His doctor recommends that he does more **exercise**.

a) Asthma is caused by over-sensitive air passages in the breathing system.
What is the name of the pair of tubes that take air into the lungs?

....

b) Tom decides to join a local gym.

   i) When he joins, the trainer asks him lots of questions about his health and lifestyle.
   Give **one** reason why it is important to ask these questions.

   ....

   ii) While Tom is exercising he hurts a muscle in his leg. Describe
   four steps the physiotherapist at the gym would use to treat Tom.

   ....

   ....

Q5 A **manager** in the **NHS** is in charge of the health care facilities in the area.

a) Describe **one** function of the National Health Service.

....

b) i) Give an example of a local organisation that provides health care.

   ....

   ii) Describe the services that this organisation would offer.

   ....

c) The health service in the area is running a campaign to promote awareness of diabetes.

   i) Give a reason why it is important to provide the public with information about health.

   ....

   ii) Part of the campaign is to offer urine tests to people who think they might have diabetes.
   Which of the following substances would the test be looking for? Circle the correct answer.

   urea   glucose   DNA   water   haemoglobin

   iii) The tests are carried out using test sticks. Give one **disadvantage** of using these over lab tests.

   ....

Module 1 — Life Care

Module 2 — Agriculture and Food

Products from Organisms

Q1 Tracey is researching **farming** in Brazil. She knows they grow bananas (which are an example of a **gathered harvest**) and potatoes (which are an example of a **whole organism** harvest).

a) Explain the difference between a gathered harvest and a whole organism harvest.

....

....

b) Complete the table below using the words provided.

food from microorganisms   milk   fruits   meats   vegetables

sugar beet   wool   crops   nuts   extracellular protein from microorganisms

Gathered harvests	Whole organism harvests

Q2 **Organisms** are also used to make other useful products.

a) Give **one** example of how microorganisms are used in food processing.

....

b) Give **one** example of how plants are used to make fuel.

....

....

Top Tips: Agriculture is really important in the UK. A lot of the food we eat in this country is grown in this country, which means it takes a lot of people and a lot of space to produce it all.

Module 2 — Agriculture and Food

Agriculture in the UK

Q1 Joe works on a large **arable** farm.

a) Circle the correct word(s) to complete the sentences about arable farming.

  i) Arable farming involves growing **crops** / **animals** for consumption.

  ii) Arable farming products can also be used for other things like making **milk products** / **biofuel**.

b) What are the other **four** main areas of agriculture in the UK?

  1. ....   2. ....

  3. ....   4. ....

c) The table opposite shows how many hours Joe spends on the different tasks listed, in one year.

  i) Complete the table by calculating how many hours Joe spends harvesting in a year.

  ii) List two jobs Joe may have to do that would be included in 'looking after the crops'.

  1. ....

  2. ....

Work Done	Time (hours)
Ploughing and planting	144
Looking after the crops	720
Harvesting	
Other	576
Total	1 800

Q2 The structure of the UK **egg industry** has changed in recent years. The table below shows the percentages of the egg market represented by three methods of chicken farming — **laying** (battery hens), **barn** (hens that roam freely indoors) and **free range** (hens that can roam freely outdoors).

Year	Percentage of egg market for each type of chicken farming		
	Laying	Barn	Free range
1999	78	6	16
2005	66	7	27

Key:
- Laying
- Free Range
- Barn

a) Use the figures above to complete the bar chart. The data for 1999 has been plotted for you.

b) Which type of chicken farming has increased the most between 1999 and 2005?

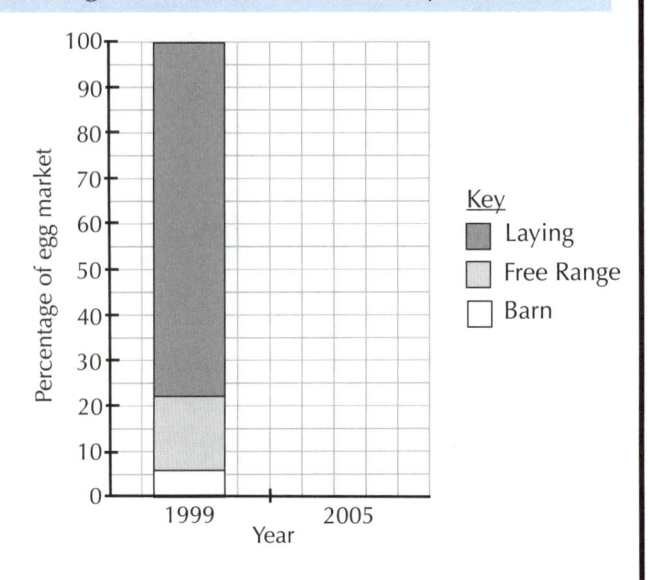

....

c) Raising hens and collecting eggs are jobs in which area of agriculture? Circle the correct answer.

  Horticulture   Dairy farming   Poultry farming

Module 2 — Agriculture and Food

Agriculture in the UK

Q3 Muhya is a **butcher**. Her job involves preparing cuts of meat and selling them to customers.

a) What is meant by **the chain of food production**?

....

b) What stage of the chain of food production is Muhya involved in?

....

Q4 **Milkmen** deliver fresh milk to customers' homes every morning.

a) Complete the paragraph on milk production using the words given below.

delivers   dairy   transported   stored   bottling   processed   pasteurising

.... cattle are milked every day on farms.

The milk is .... from farms to a dairy for processing.

This includes .... and ....

The .... milk is sent to local centres where it may be

.... until it's needed. The milkman collects the milk from

the distribution centre and .... it to his customers.

b) Biotechnology is used to make cheese from milk.
Give **one** other use of biotechnology in food production.

....

Q5 Tasty Tea is a specialist tea company that produces flavoured tea bags. The tea is **processed** in Cumbria from **tea leaves** hand-picked in India.

Draw lines to match each description below to the correct stage in the chain of food production.

Packets of tea bags are sent out to shops for sale	Growing
Tea bushes are grown on plantations in India	Transporting
Packets of tea bags are kept at the Tasty Tea's distribution centre	Processing
The tea leaves are made into packets of flavoured tea bags	Storing
Picked tea leaves are shipped to the UK and driven to Cumbria	Delivering

Module 2 — Agriculture and Food

Regulating Agriculture and Food

Q1 Haile works for an organisation that is involved in the **regulation** of agriculture and food production in the UK.

   a) Suggest the names of **two** organisations Haile might work for.

      1. ....

      2. ....

   b) Agriculture is regulated for three important reasons.
Tick the **three** correct boxes below to show what these reasons are.

      For public health and safety ☐

      To protect the rights of shop keepers ☐

      For animal welfare ☐

      To protect homeowners ☐

      To protect supermarket interests ☐

      To protect the environment ☐

   c) Name **two** organisations that support a part of the food industry and help to promote its products.

      1. ....

      2. ....

Q2 Jeanette is an **enforcement officer**. She monitors restaurants to make sure they are following **health and safety regulations**.

Complete the paragraph below using the words provided.

| rules | environmental health | hygiene | monitor | pollution | chain |

Enforcement officers make sure .... and regulations are followed by everyone who works in the .... of food production. Factory inspectors .... workplaces and make sure people are abiding by safety rules. .... practitioners visit places where food is produced or served to make sure that good health and .... practices are being followed. They also help to protect the environment, e.g. by measuring .... levels.

Module 2 — Agriculture and Food

Products from Plants

Q1 Fraser grows **plants** on his farm. The produce he harvests is either **eaten** by himself or his farm animals or is used to make **other food products**.

a) Complete the table below using the words provided.

sugar   silage   potatoes   flour   vegetable oil   hay   lettuce   apples   grass

Food for farm animals	Food for humans	Food ingredients

b) Lots of other useful products can be made from plants.
Give **one** example of a product made from plants for each of the categories below.

i) Fibres or fabric ....

ii) Biofuels ....

iii) Other materials ....

Q2 'The Sweetest Thing' process and package **sugar** for a major supermarket chain. The diagram below shows the stages involved in processing sugar beet to make sugar.

a) Why are the sugar beet chips pressed?

....

....

b) Why is the water evaporated?

....

....

....

The sugar beet is harvested → The sugar beet is cut into chips → The chips are added to water tanks and left to soak → The chips are taken out of the water tanks and pressed → The water is evaporated away by boiling → The sugar is dried and packaged

---

Top Tips: Plants are really very handy things. We make loads of different products from them, not to mention all the different plants we eat. In the exam you could be asked to interpret information about the stages involved in processing a food product, like sugar, flour or vegetable oil.

Module 2 — Agriculture and Food

The Plant Life-Cycle

Q1 Rio works at a nursery where he **breeds** new fruit varieties with interesting colours and flavours.

Draw lines to match each stage in the life cycle of a fruiting plant with the correct description.

Pollination	The male and female sex cells join together
Fertilisation	The seed starts to grow into a new plant
Production of fruit	The fruit may be eaten by animals and the seeds scattered in their poo
Dispersal	The seed is formed and a fruit develops around it
Germination	Pollen is transferred to the female part of the flower

Q2 **Agricultural scientists** study the effects of temperature on **seed germination**.

a) Number the boxes below (1-4) to show the correct order of the germination of a seed.

- Extra roots grow and the first green leaves appear. ☐
- The radicle splits the outer coat and begins to grow into the soil. ☐
- The seed takes in water. ☐
- The plumule begins to grow up through the soil. ☐

b) Name **two** conditions that are required for a seed to start germinating.

1. ....
2. ....

Q3 Erik is a **farmer**. This year he's going to plant some cucumbers, which he has never grown before. A local seed supplier sends him the information on the right about three types of **seed** they sell.

Seed type	Fruit colour	Fruit taste	% germination rate
A	Light green	Sweet	75
B	Bluey green	Slightly sweet	78
C	Bottle green	Slightly bitter	84

Erik doesn't mind what colour his cucumbers are or how sweet they are. He wants to produce the greatest number of plants from the fewest number of seeds. Which seed type should he buy?

....

Module 2 — Agriculture and Food

Plant Growth

Q1 Ankit is an **agricultural consultant** who advises farmers on how to increase crop yield. He says that sunlight is very important because plants produce their own '**food**' using **sunlight**.

  a) What is the name of the process that plants use to produce their own food?

  ....

  b) Complete the word equation for this process using the words given below.

  carbon dioxide   chlorophyll   glucose

  $$.................... + \text{water} \xrightarrow{\text{sunlight}} \text{oxygen} + ...$$

Q2 Farmer Stubbs is learning about the things that her crops need to **grow**.

  a) Complete the passage below by choosing words from the list. Words can be used once or not at all.

  chlorophyll   soil   green   oxygen   water   glucose
  blue   carbon dioxide   energy   light   chloroplasts

  .... enters leaves from the surrounding air. ....
  is drawn up from the .... from the Sun
  provides ...., which is absorbed by the ....
  pigment called ...., found in ....

  b) Suggest **one** place where Farmer Stubbs could grow her crops that would allow her to artificially create the ideal conditions for photosynthesis.

  ....

Top Tips: The carbon dioxide needed for photosynthesis is taken in through the leaves and the oxygen produced is **released** through them too. So plants, being as clever as they are, have leaves that are specially adapted to allow good gaseous exchange. Handy.

Module 2 — Agriculture and Food

Plant Growth

Q3 Richard grows houseplants **commercially** to sell to garden centres. Over the years Richard has spent a lot of money building **glasshouses** in which to grow his plants.

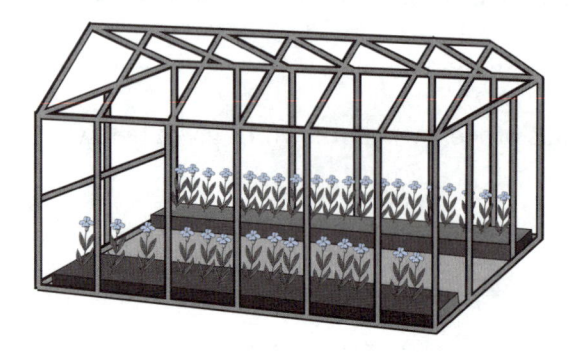

a) Richard **burns fuel** in his glasshouses to help his plants grow.

  i) As well as releasing heat, what does burning fuel produce that helps plants to grow?

  ....

  ii) Why does this product help Richard's plants to grow?

  ....

  Think about what plants need to make their own food.

  ....

  ....

b) Richard's glasshouses also have **artificial lighting**.

  i) When would Richard use the artificial lighting?

  ....

  ii) Explain how using artificial lighting helps plants to grow more.

  ....

  ....

c) Describe another benefit of growing plants in glasshouses.

  ....

Top Tips: Gardeners (and farmers) use glasshouses because they can create ideal conditions for plant growth, helping them maximise their profits. Make sure you know how gardeners can provide plants with light, carbon dioxide and heat by artificial means.

Module 2 — Agriculture and Food

Crop Yield

Q1 Asik is a strawberry farmer. He uses pesticides to help increase his **crop yield**.

Give **two** ways that pests can reduce crop yields.

1. ....

2. ....

Q2 Nadia is an **agricultural scientist**. She carries out an experiment to see which of three fertilizers increases the **crop yield** of pea plants the most.

a) How can pea crop yield be measured?

....

b) Nadia grows twelve different pea plants from seeds. She grows three with each of the three different fertilizers and three control plants with no added fertilizer. She measures the crop yield of each pea plant and then calculates an average for each set of plants. Her results are given in the table below.

	No fertilizer	Fertilizer A	Fertilizer B	Fertilizer C
Average mass of peas per plant (g)	50	62	55	74

i) Complete the bar chart of Nadia's results by drawing the two missing bars.

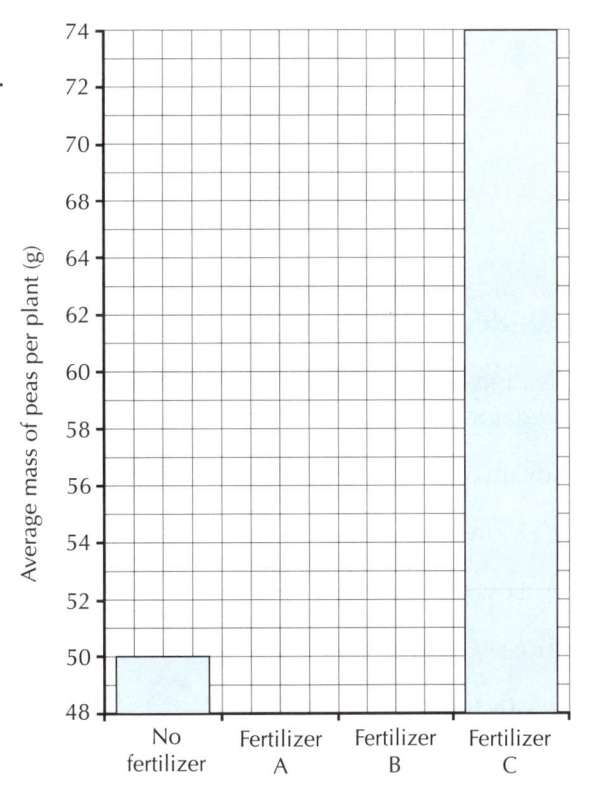

ii) Which of the fertilizers used in the experiment was most effective in increasing crop yield? How can you tell?

....

....

Module 2 — Agriculture and Food

Crop Yield

Q3 Bio-Control supply **predator organisms** to help control pests. Jacob contacts Bio-Control to see if they can help protect his prizewinning roses from **aphids** (little green pests that damage roses).

Jacob carries out an experiment to see which method of pest control works the best. He uses the predator organisms and two different pesticides in separate glasshouses. Aphids damage developing rose buds, preventing them from opening. Jacob counts the number of developing rose buds and the number that open to form flowers. His results are shown below.

	Predator organism	Pesticide A	Pesticide B
Number of rose buds	300	300	300
Number of rose buds that opened	242	238	278
Percentage that opened	81%		

a) Complete the table by calculating the percentage of rose buds that opened in the glasshouses where pesticide A and B were used.

b) Which type of pest control was the most effective?

....

c) Suggest how Jacob could have included a control in the experiment.

....

Q4 Ashmi grows flowering plants, which she sells to garden centres. Ashmi usually uses **pesticides** in her glasshouses but she has started looking into using **predator organisms**.

Tick the boxes to show whether the advantages and disadvantages below refer to predator organisms or chemical control.

a) Advantages

                                                              Predator Chemical

    i) More cost efficient

    ii) Less polluting

    iii) Easy to apply to all plants

b) Disadvantages   **Predator Chemical**

    i) Won't kill all pests

    ii) Requires management and training

    iii) Could kill harmless or beneficial insects

Growing Plants

Q1 Geoff has a market stall where he sells crops grown on his small farm. He knows he needs to provide certain things for his plants get high **crop yields**.

a) Complete the passage below by circling the correct word(s) from each pair.

Plants need certain things to grow. This includes **hydroponics** / **nutrients**,

the right **pH** / **oxygen content** and water, which is needed for **photosynthesis** / **respiration**.

b) Geoff's friend, Darren, grows tomatoes using **hydroponics**.

i) What does 'hydroponics' mean?

....

ii) List **two advantages** and **two disadvantages** of using hydroponics to grow plants.

Advantages ....

....

Disadvantages ....

....

Q2 Joe grows vegetables in his back garden. He adds **compost** to his soil once a year after he has harvested his vegetables. The graph below shows the **mineral content** of his soil over a year.

a) Joe plants his vegetables in January (**A**) and harvests them in July (**B**). Describe the trend shown on the graph between points **A** and **B**.

....

....

....

b) Why does Joe add compost to his soil?

....

....

c) In which month did Joe add compost to the soil? Explain your answer.

....

....

Module 2 — Agriculture and Food

Cuttings and Tissue Culture

Q1 Hiroshi works for an **agricultural** firm that produces **genetically identical maize plants** by tissue culture. The diagram below shows this process.

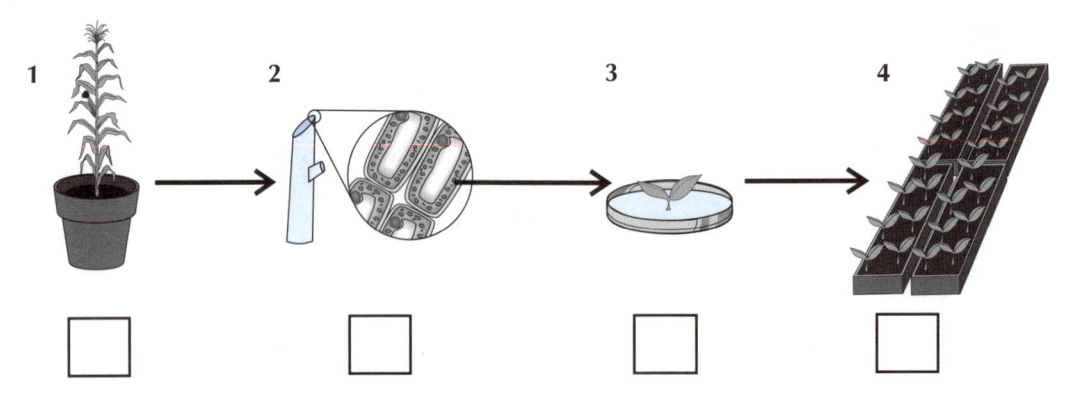

1 → 2 → 3 → 4

☐   ☐   ☐   ☐

a) Match the statements below to the stages in the diagram by writing each letter in the correct box.

A Cells removed from growing tip.

B Clones grown in potting compost.

C Parent plant with desired characteristics chosen.

D Cells placed on sterile growing substance containing hormones.

b) The company produces 50,000 maize plants per year. Using tissue culture methods, each plant costs 3p to produce. Using traditional methods, each plant would cost 7p to produce.

i) How much does the company save per year by using tissue culture rather than traditional methods?

....

ii) Describe the 'traditional' method of producing genetically identical plants.

....

Q2 Clive farms **African Violets**. Last year he produced a **new breed** with very large flowers that won a national flower prize. He decides to produce some **genetically identical plants** from his prizewinning violet.

a) Tick the correct boxes to show whether each of the following statements about producing genetically identical plants is true or false.

True   False

It's hard to fertilise the plants   ☐   ☐

It's possible to mass-produce plants that are hard to grow from seed   ☐   ☐

The main disadvantage is a reduced gene pool   ☐   ☐

b) Circle the correct word to complete the sentence below.

A reduced gene pool means there are fewer different **alleles** / **plants** in a population.

Module 2 — Agriculture and Food

Products from Animals

Q1 Laura owns a small **arable farm**. She is thinking of expanding her farm to include **animals**.

a) Complete the table using some of the words given below, to show the types of products that can be made from **animals**. Words can be used once or not at all.

silage   leather   dairy products   wool   meat   tomatoes   manure   cotton   bonemeal

Food from animals	Textiles from animals	Fertilizers from animals

b) To increase her profits Laura needs her animals to grow as much as possible. List **four** factors that affect animal growth.

1. ....   2. ....

3. ....   4. ....

Q2 Nina has inherited a pig farm from her grandfather. The farm has **80 pig pens** and each pen is **100 m²**. At the moment **20 pigs** are kept in each pen. Nina researches pig farming methods and finds some guidelines stating that every pig needs at least **1 m²** of space.

a) What is the **maximum** number of pigs Nina could keep in each pen?

....

b) A local farmer tells Nina that if she keeps the pigs in small cages she will **increase** her **meat production**. Explain why this method increases meat production.

....

....

c) Nina makes a profit of **£2** for each pig she sends to be slaughtered.

i) How much profit would she make at the moment if she sent all her pigs to be slaughtered?

....

....

ii) If Nina bought more pigs and kept **50** pigs in each of the farm's 80 pens, how much more profit would she make if she sent them all to be slaughtered?

....

....

Module 2 — Agriculture and Food

Intensive and Organic Farming

Q1 Some farmers are changing from **intensive farming** methods to **organic methods**.

a) Draw lines to match the statements below to show the **advantages** of organic farming.

Fewer artificial pesticides are used — animals have more room to move.

No battery farming — there is less risk of chemicals remaining on food.

b) Complete the paragraph below about organic farming by circling the correct word in each pair.

Organic farming requires **less / more** space than intensive farming. It is **more / less** labour-intensive, which **increases / decreases** production costs. Overall, organic farming produces **less / more** food than intensive farming for the same area of land.

Q2 The table below shows the amount of **energy** that two farmers put **into** their farms over a year, for activities like ploughing. It also shows the **energy** content of the food harvested at the end of the year. One farm is an **intensive** farm and one farm is an **organic** farm. They both produce cereals.

	Energy input (MJ per hectare)	Food energy output (MJ per hectare)
Intensive Farm	12 000	4 000
Organic Farm	3 500	1 900

1 MJ = a million joules

a) How much more energy did the intensive farmer put into his farm per hectare compared to the organic farmer?

....

b) How much more food energy did the intensive farmer get out of his farm per hectare compared to the organic farmer?

....

c) The intensive farm also raises chickens. Give **one** ethical concern about intensive farming of chickens.

....

....

Simon's farming methods were intense

Top Tips: In the exam they might ask you to compare different farming methods. You also need to know the ethical concerns about intensive farming inside out.

Module 2 — Agriculture and Food

Sexual Reproduction in Animals

Q1 Nadine works for a company that supplies sperm from bulls for use in the **artificial insemination** of cows.

a) Draw lines to match each stage in sexual reproduction in mammals to the correct description.

Formation of gametes	The fetus grows during pregnancy
Fertilisation	The baby grows into an adult mammal
Internal development	The male and female sex cells join together
Birth	The sex cells are formed
Growth and development	The baby is born

How you doing?

b) Complete the paragraph on artificial insemination using the words given below.

fertilisation, an egg, desirable, meat, pipette, temperature, frozen

The first step in artificial insemination is the selection of animals with .... characteristics, e.g. high .... or milk yields. The sperm is collected in a device that keeps it at the right .... The sperm is checked for quality and is stored in plastic straws, which can be .... for later use. To inseminate the female a long .... is used to insert the contents of the sperm. It's important to inseminate the female at the right time, just as she is about to release ...., to increase the chances of ....

Q2 Christopher owns a **cattle farm**. He wants to artificially inseminate some of his cows. He receives the following information on available sperm stocks.

Christopher is not interested in winning any competitions with his animals. Which bull's sperm should he buy?

....

Bull	Prizes won	Meat yield	Health
A	None	High	Average
B	None	High	Good
C	Best-in-show, 2006	Medium	Good

Module 2 — Agriculture and Food

Sexual Reproduction in Animals

Q3 Tom breeds **pigs**. He specialises in creating new breeds for meat production.

a) Describe how artificial insemination would be used to breed pigs with high meat yields.

....

....

b) Suggest **two** advantages of using artificial insemination in pig farming.

1. ....

2. ....

c) Circle **two** characteristics that Tom may want his pigs to have.

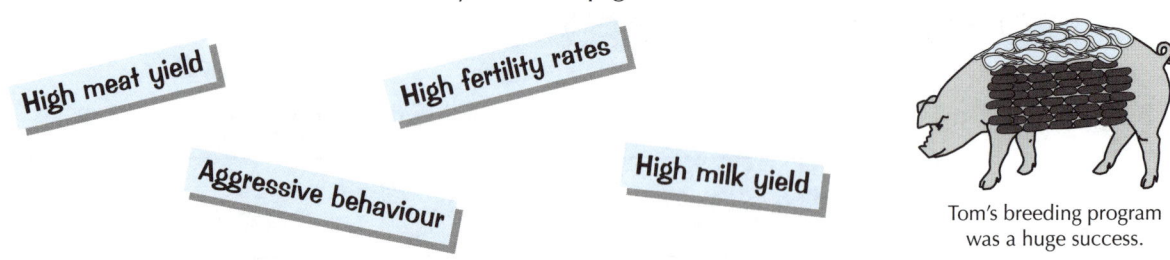

High meat yield

High fertility rates

Aggressive behaviour

High milk yield

Tom's breeding program was a huge success.

Q4 The bar chart below shows the average **meat yield** for the offspring of three different bulls. The table shows the **fertility information** for the same three bulls.

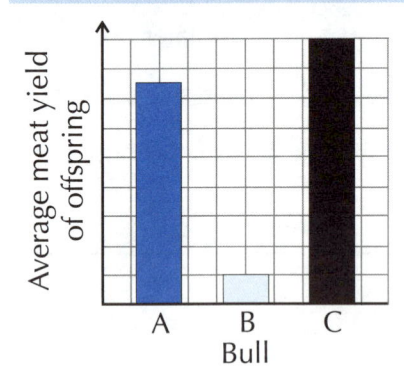

Bull	Number of times sperm artificially inseminated	Number of offspring born from artificial insemination	Fertility rate (%)
A	230	210	
B	230	227	99%
C	230	123	

a) Calculate the fertility rate of bull A and C.

b) Which bull's sperm would be the most useful for the production of beef cattle using artificial insemination? Explain why.

....

....

Top Tips: So, if you wanted to take over the world using goldfish, you'd probably want to use sperm from the more aggressive goldfish with long memories, rather than the dappy ones that just idly swim around in a circle all day long. (You can tell which ones are aggressive — they bite.)

Module 2 — Agriculture and Food

Selective Breeding and Embryo Transplants

Q1 Jeremy is a beef farmer. To maximise his profits he **selectively breeds** cows that have the highest meat yields.

  a) Number the sentences below to show the stages of selective breeding in the correct order.

   ☐ Breed them with each other.
   ☐ Select the best offspring.
   ☐ Continue the process over many generations.
   ☐ Combine with the best you already have and breed again.
   [1] Select individuals with the best characteristics.

  b) Complete the following sentences by circling the correct word(s) in each pair.

   i) Selective breeding can **increase / decrease** the number of different alleles in a population.

   ii) Animals in a herd that have all been bred selectively will be **closely / distantly** related.

   iii) If a new disease appears **few / all** of the animals are likely to be affected.

   iv) Selective breeding leads to **an increase / a decrease** in the gene pool.

Q2 Clive **farms** two small **beef herds**. Herd A is made up entirely of offspring that were cloned using **embryo transplantation**. Traditional **selective breeding** techniques were used to produce herd B.

  a) Describe the steps involved in embryo transplantation.

   ....
   ....
   ....
   ....

  b) Give **one** disadvantage of using embryo transplantation.

   ....
   ....

  c) Tick the boxes to say whether the following apply to herd A, herd B or neither.

	A	B	Neither
i) The offspring are clones of each other.	☐	☐	☐
ii) The offspring are clones of their mother.	☐	☐	☐
iii) The offspring are genetically different from their parents and each other.	☐	☐	☐

Module 2 — Agriculture and Food

Products from Microorganisms

Q1 Amy works in **food production**. She is developing new ways of using **microorganisms** in food production.

a) Give **one** example of a type of alcohol and **one** example of a food product that are made using microorganisms.

i) Alcohol ....

ii) Food ....

b) Amy is trying to modify a microorganism so that it will produce a useful protein.

i) What is this process called? Circle the correct answer.

mycoprotein modification   respiration   genetic modification   fermentation

ii) Name **one** protein that is produced using this method.

....

Q2 **Yeast** is a microorganism that makes bread **rise** so that it's light and fluffy.

a) Circle the correct word(s) in each pair to complete the following passage about microorganisms.

> Microorganisms use **photosynthesis / respiration** to release **energy / oxygen** from **sugars / salts**. This process is also known as **distillation / fermentation**.

b) Name **two** types of microorganisms, other than yeast.

1. ....   2. ....

c) **Anaerobic** fermentation by yeast causes bread to rise. Use the words given below to complete the equation for anaerobic respiration in yeast. Words can be used once or not at all.

carbon dioxide   water   lactic acid   ethanol   sugar   glucose

.... → .... + ...

d) Name another useful product that can be made using yeast.

Think about what drinks yeast is used to make.

....

Top Tips:
Microorganisms aren't the only things that can respire anaerobically — if you hold both arms out from your sides for as long as you can, your shoulders start to 'burn'. That's because your muscles start respiring anaerobically, producing lactic acid, which causes the pain.

Module 2 — Agriculture and Food

Products from Microorganisms

Q3 Some **vegetarians** eat a meat substitute made from **mycoprotein**.

The diagram opposite shows a fermenter that can be used for producing mycoprotein. The microorganisms respire **aerobically** during mycoprotein production.

a) Explain the purpose of the air supply.

....

....

....

b) Before fermentation begins, the fermenter is usually filled with **steam** and then cooled. Suggest why this is done.

....

....

c) What type of microorganism is used to make mycoprotein?

....

Q4 Chris is learning about the **cheese-making process**.

a) Circle the correct word to complete the sentence below.

Anaerobic fermentation by **bacteria** / **yeast** is used when making cheese.

b) Tick the box to show which statement best describes anaerobic fermentation.

When microorganisms respire in the absence of oxygen. ☐

When microorganisms respire in the presence of oxygen. ☐

c) Write out the word equation for the anaerobic respiration used in cheese making.

....

Q5 Write the word equation for aerobic respiration.

....

Top Tips: Microorganisms aren't just used to **make** mycoprotein, they **are** the actual mycoprotein. They're grown in huge fermenters and their biomass is used to make substitute meat.

Module 2 — Agriculture and Food

Products from Microorganisms

Q6 A **biotechnology company** wants to expand the number of substances it produces from **genetically modified organisms**. Protein X is used in food manufacturing to prevent decay.

Put the following sentences (A-D) in the correct order to describe how protein X is produced from genetically modified microorganisms.

    A The product is collected and purified for use.

    B The microorganism is grown so there are millions of them.

    C The gene for protein X is selected.

    D The gene for protein X is added to the genetic material of a microorganism.

Correct Order — ....

Q7 **Yogtastic** is a Cornish **yoghurt manufacturer** that wants to increase its national sales by improving its **website**. The owners think that an **explanation** of how yoghurt is made might encourage people to buy their products **on line**.

The diagram below shows the stages involved in producing yoghurt.

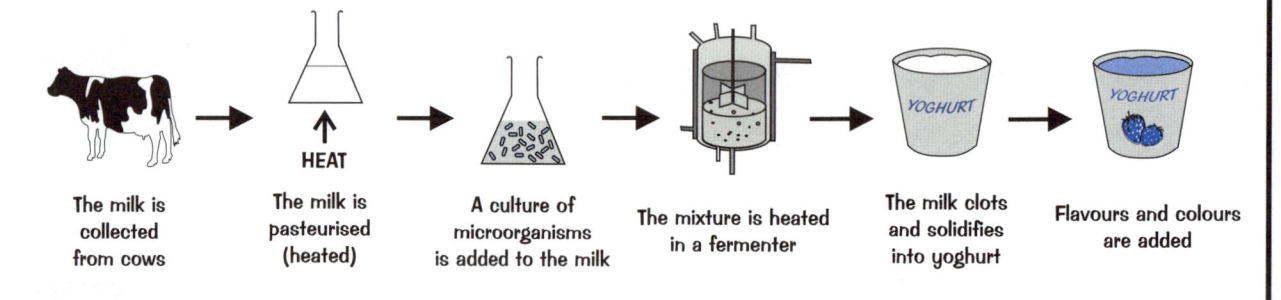

The milk is collected from cows → The milk is pasteurised (heated) → A culture of microorganisms is added to the milk → The mixture is heated in a fermenter → The milk clots and solidifies into yoghurt → Flavours and colours are added

a) Why is the milk **pasteurised**?

....

b) What type of microorganism is added to the milk? Circle the correct answer.

    yeast   viruses   bacteria   fungi

c) The microorganisms convert sugar in the milk into lactic acid. What is this process called?

....

Module 2 — Agriculture and Food

Growth of Microorganisms

Q1 Amar tests some samples from a **food factory** for the presence of **microorganisms** that can cause **food spoilage**.

a) Explain how microorganisms can cause food spoilage.

....

....

b) Amar uses **aseptic techniques** when testing his samples.
Why does he use aseptic techniques? Tick the correct statement.

To make sure things are measured correctly ☐

To prevent contamination ☐

To kill any microorganisms in his sample ☐

c) Circle the correct word to complete the following sentence.

All / some / no microorganisms cause disease.

Q2 Charlotte is growing some microorganisms to produce **extracellular protein**. She checks the **growth rate** of the microorganisms by measuring the **turbidity** of the liquid they are growing in.

a) What does turbidity mean?

....

b) Charlotte removes a sample from the growth mixture every hour for 14 hours and records its turbidity. The graph shows how the turbidity changes.

i) Describe the trend shown by the graph.

....

....

ii) During which period does the **maximum** rate of growth occur? Circle the correct answer.

0-2 hours   4-6 hours   6-8 hours

c) Charlotte carries out a **colony count** on the sample removed after 2 hours. Her plate is shown on the right. How many microorganisms were in the sample?

....

d) Suggest another method of measuring the population growth of microorganisms.

....

Module 2 — Agriculture and Food

Testing Food

Q1 Wayne works in a **brewery**. It's his job to decide when **fermentation** is complete and the beer is ready to be processed and packaged for sale.

   a) i) By looking at the beer, how can Wayne tell when fermentation is complete?

   ....

   ii) Looking at the beer to see if it is ready is an example of what type of test? Circle the correct answer.

   Qualitative   Semi-quantitative   Quantitative

   b) Wayne measures the exact level of alcohol in the beer using a hydrometer. What type of test is this?

   ....

Q2 Sharon is a **butcher**. She keeps her meat in freezers and chilled cabinets before selling it. She sometimes sends samples of her meat away to be tested for the presence of **bacteria**.

   Sharon sends a sample from the same piece of meat, kept in her chiller cabinet, to be examined each day for seven days. The results are shown in the bar chart below.

   a) What do the results show?

   ....

   ....

   b) Line X shows the amount of bacteria that would cause the meat to be regarded as **unsafe** to eat.

   i) A customer buys some of the meat on **day 2** and stores it in his fridge. What is the maximum number of days he can keep the meat before eating it? Circle the correct answer.

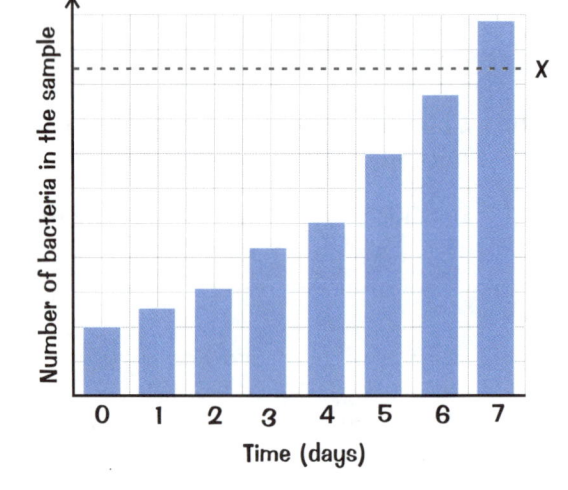

   1 day   4 days   6 days

   ii) Sharon tells a customer she can keep the meat in a fridge for **three** days before it needs to be eaten. On what day did this customer buy her meat? Circle the correct answer.

   Day 1   Day 3   Day 7   Day 6

Top Tips: Remember to learn some different examples of food tests. You need to know some that are qualitative — you can test by simply **looking**, semi-quantitative — gives an **estimate** of safety or quality, and quantitative — gives an **accurate measurement** of safety or quality.

Module 2 — Agriculture and Food

Testing Food

Q3 Some **plum trees** grow best in slightly **acidic** soil.

Circle the correct word(s) in each pair to complete the sentences below.

a) Using pH paper would be a **qualitative** / **semi-quantitative** way to test the pH of soil.

b) To get a more precise reading a pH meter could be used, which is a **quantitative** / **qualitative** method of testing soil pH.

Q4 José grows **grapes** in Spain and sells them to a large supermarket chain in the UK. He is testing different **transportation methods** to see which is the best way to transport his grapes.

The pictures below show two sets of José's grapes when they arrived in the UK. One set was sent in unchilled cargo boxes on a boat. The other was sent on an aeroplane in chilled boxes.

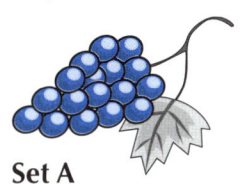

Set A    Set B

a) Which set of grapes appears to be **spoiled**?

....

b) Visually examining the grapes for spoilage is an example of what kind of test?

....

c) Draw lines to link the set of grapes to the method of transportation used to send them to the UK.

Set A   Boat

Set B   Aeroplane

Q5 Milktastic make **flavoured milkshakes** for UK supermarkets. They are testing a new ingredient that should **reduce the growth rate** of any **bacteria** in the milkshake.

They monitor the amount of bacteria present in a sample of milkshake every day for a week. The results are shown opposite.

a) Does the new ingredient work?

....

b) Line X shows the number of bacteria that would be regarded as **unsafe**. After how many days would milkshake with the new ingredient be unsafe? ....

Module 2 — Agriculture and Food

The Food Market

Q1 Carmel works for **The British Potato Council**. She researches the **food market** to assess the demand for potatoes and to find out about any changes to agricultural policies that may affect the potato industry.

   a) Complete the paragraph below by filling in the blanks using the words provided.

> selling   demand   supply   buying   price

The food market is made up of everyone .... and .... food products. The amount of a product that is available to buy is described as .... The amount of product that people want to buy is known as .... Supply and demand both affect the .... of products.

   b) The Government can influence the prices of some food products by giving **subsidies** (extra money) to the producers.

Circle the correct word to complete the following sentence.

Government subsidies can keep the **price** / **size** of certain products **higher** / **lower** than it would be otherwise.

Q2 **The British Egg Information Service** helps to **market** UK eggs and egg products.

   a) Tick the boxes to show whether the following statements are true or false.

	True	False
Advertising isn't important in marketing a product	☐	☐
Marketing lets people know what products are available to buy	☐	☐
Many producers use advertising to market their products	☐	☐
Marketing reduces the cost of products	☐	☐

   b) Some eggs and egg boxes display a **quality mark** from the British Egg Information Service. What does a quality mark tell you about a product?

....

   c) Why might it be beneficial to a company for their product to carry a quality mark?

....

Module 2 — Agriculture and Food

Sustainable Agriculture

Q1 Hafiz works for Defra. He helps to promote the use of **sustainable farming techniques** in the UK.

Circle the correct word(s) to complete the sentence below.

> Sustainable agriculture is living / farming in a way that allows waste / food from crops and livestock / pets to be produced indefinitely without damaging the environment / machinery.

Q2 James is an **agricultural adviser**. He knows that plants grow best in good quality soil that is filled with nutrients, including nitrogen compounds. He advises farmers to grow **legume plants** in fields **after** other crops have been harvested. Legume plants return nitrogen compounds to the soil.

a) Suggest why it would help farmers to plant legumes after harvesting other crops.

....

The graph shows how the level of nitrogen compounds in the soil in a field changes with time.

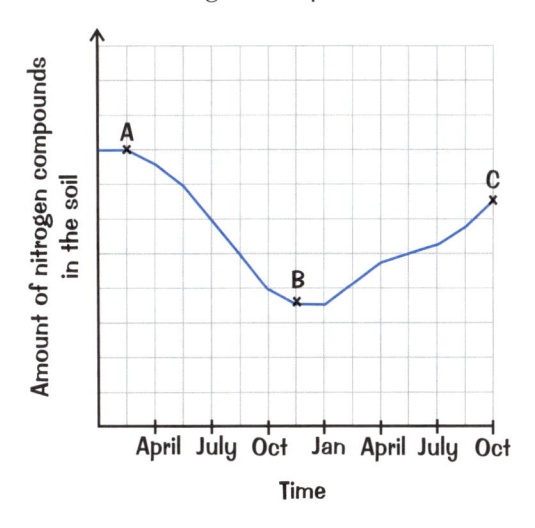

b) i) What trend does the graph show between points A and B?

....

ii) What trend does the graph show between points B and C?

....

c) **Legume plants** and **leeks** have both been grown in the field, at different times. Draw lines to link each plant with when it was grown in the field.

| Legume | | Between points A and B |
| Leeks | | Between points B and C |

Sustainable Agriculture

Q3 Kevin owns a large **farm** in Cumbria. He is trying to run the farm sustainably.

Suggest **two** steps Kevin could take to reduce the farm's dependency on non-renewable resources.

1. ....

2. ....

Q4 Karen is an **agricultural scientist**. She is carrying out an experiment to see if growing different plants in the same field can reduce pest problems.

She plants carrots and onions in three fields and only carrots in three other fields. Her results are given in the table below.

	Carrots and onions	Carrots only
Number of carrots planted	10 000	10 000
Number of carrots damaged by pests	Field 1 — 1650 Field 2 — 92 Field 3 — 765	Field 1 — 1919 Field 2 — 815 Field 3 — 3789
Average number of carrots damaged by pests	836	

a) Complete the table by calculating the average number of carrots damaged per field in the carrots only fields.

b) Draw a bar chart to show this data, using the axes provided.

c) i) In which type of field were the least number of crops lost to pests?

....

ii) In which type of field would less pesticide be needed?

....

d) Using less pesticide is a move towards sustainable agriculture. Why? Tick the **two** correct boxes.

- It reduces the use of non-renewable resources that are used to make pesticides ☐
- It increases the use of renewable resources ☐
- It could reduce the harmful effects of using pesticides on the environment ☐
- It could reduce the amount of pests killed by pesticides ☐

Top Tips: Some people think fish farms are a good way to help to move towards sustainable fishing — it helps to conserve wild fish stocks and to prevent overfishing of the oceans.

Module 2 — Agriculture and Food

Mixed Questions for Module 2

Q1 Abdullah is a farmer. He grows **wheat crops** that are processed into flour.

   a) What type of harvest is wheat an example of? Circle the correct answer.

       gathered   whole organism

   b) Growing food crops is part of which type of agriculture?

      ....

The table below gives some data about how much flour and bread can be produced from one bushel of wheat. A bushel is a unit of measurement.

   c) Abdullah's field can produce 37 bushels of wheat. Calculate:

	From one bushel
Mass of wheat (kg)	27
Mass of flour (kg)	19
Number of loaves of bread	70

      i) The amount of flour, in kg, that can be produced from one field of wheat.

          ....

          ....

      ii) The number of loaves of bread that can be produced from one field of wheat.

          ....

Q2 Busy-Bees **nursery** specialises in breeding and selling **orchids**. They sell seeds and fully grown plants of all their varieties.

   a) Suggest **one** way that Busy-Bees can make genetically identical plants of their best-selling varieties.

      ....

   b) Below is some information on the different orchid seeds that Busy-Bees sell.

Seed	Flower colour	Percentage germination rate	Flower size
A	Purple	84	Large
B	Mixed	85	Medium
C	Mixed	96	Medium

Dave has a large garden that he wants to fill with a mixture of colours. He needs to produce lots of plants from the fewest number of seeds. Sharon wants large, purple flowers. Suggest a suitable seed type for:

      i) Dave ....   **ii)** Sharon ....

Module 2 — Agriculture and Food

Mixed Questions for Module 2

Q3 Dave's bakery only uses **eggs** from **organically** farmed hens.

a) Suggest **one** job that may be carried out on a poultry farm.

....

b) Dave won't use eggs from intensively farmed hens because of the ethical issues involved. Give **two** ethical concerns about intensive farming.

1. ....

2. ....

Q4 Henry works on a small **farm**, picking **cherries**.

Henry picks some cherries and puts them in the farm shop for sale. After three days the cherries that hadn't been sold looked spoiled. The cherries are shown on the right.

a) How can you tell the cherries are spoiled? Tick the one correct answer.

- They are smaller than normal cherries ☐
- You can see the waste products produced by microorganisms ☐
- You can see the visible growth of microorganisms ☐

b) Some of the cherries are used to make cherry wine.

i) What type of microorganism is used to make alcohol? Circle the correct answer.

bacteria   yeast   viruses

ii) Name the **two** products of anaerobic respiration in this microorganism.

1. .... 2. ....

Q5 An **agricultural consultant** goes to a local **cattle farm** to offer some practical advice about raising animals.

a) Give **two** products that come from cattle.

1. .... 2. ....

b) The farm uses selective breeding within the herd. The consultant advises them that selective breeding can have disadvantages. Give **one** disadvantage of selective breeding.

....

Module 2 — Agriculture and Food

Mixed Questions for Module 2

Q6 Carley is an **agricultural scientist**. Her job involves testing very old seed stocks to see if they will germinate.

Carley has some seeds from a plant that is endangered. She carries out an investigation on a small number of the seeds to see what temperature is needed for them to germinate.

a) Suggest **two** things, other than a suitable temperature, that seeds need to germinate.

1. .... 2. ....

Carley measures the **germination rate** of the seeds at six different temperatures. Her results are shown in the table below.

Temperature (°C)	Germination rate (%)
10	65
12	78
14	90
16	92
18	81
20	70

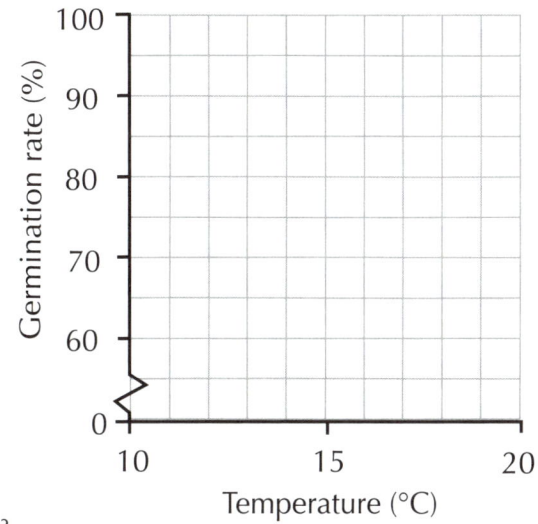

b) Draw a line graph of Carley's results on the grid opposite. Join the points with a straight line.

c) Which temperature is best for these seeds to germinate? ....

d) Name **two** things that plants need to photosynthesise.

1. .... 2. ....

Q7 **Scientists** from the Food Standards Agency are investigating a case of **food poisoning** caused by some meat. They have collected some samples of meat from the **abattoir**, the local **butcher** and the **food** that caused the food poisoning.

They measure the numbers of microorganisms in each sample by **colony counting**. The results are shown on the right.

Abattoir   Butcher   Food

a) How many microorganisms did the sample collected from the food contain? ....

b) What might explain the growth of microorganisms in the food sample? Tick the correct answer.

The meat was stored incorrectly after it was bought from the butchers ☐

The meat was stored incorrectly at the abattoir ☐

The meat wasn't cooked before it was eaten ☐

Module 2 — Agriculture and Food

Module 3 — Scientific Detection

The Work of Scientific Detectives

Q1 Sachin wants to change jobs. He has identified three areas that his **science skills** are suited to — law enforcement, environmental protection and consumer protection.

    a) Suggest **one** role for a person with scientific skills in each of the areas Sachin has identified.

        i) Law enforcement ....

        ii) Environmental protection ....

        iii) Consumer protection ....

    b) Draw lines to match the following organisations with the areas identified by Sachin.

- Forensic Science Service
- Environment Agency
- Food Standards Agency

- Consumer protection
- Law enforcement
- Environmental protection

Q2 Below are some statements about the work of **crime scene investigators**.

Tick the boxes to show whether the statements are **true** or **false**.

	True	False
Crime scene investigators monitor air quality.	☐	☐
Crime scene investigators work closely with the police.	☐	☐
Crime scene investigators collect and analyse bodily fluid samples.	☐	☐
Crime scene investigators work with businesses to reduce pollution.	☐	☐
Crime scene investigators may test firearms.	☐	☐

Q3 Theo works for the **Food Standards Agency** dealing with public health and safety concerning food.

Suggest **two** tasks that Theo may carry out as part of his job.

1. ....

2. ....

Good Laboratory Practice

Q1 Janet works for the Drinking Water Inspectorate monitoring **drinking water quality**. She has to follow good laboratory practice everyday to get reliable results.

a) Complete the following passage about good laboratory practice using the words given below.

| same | contaminated | maintained | reduce | safety | training | practices |

Good laboratory practice involves using common .... and procedures, so that different scientists will all carry out the tests in the .... way. Good laboratory practice helps to .... the chances of .... samples and unreliable results. All equipment should be well .... to ensure reliable results are produced. Staff should undergo continuous .... so they know about the best standard methods available. Following health and .... regulations is also important for good laboratory practice.

b) Circle the correct word(s) to complete the sentence about reliable results.

A set of results could be considered more reliable if the experiment had been repeated by **different** / **the same** people and the **methods** / **results** are **the same** / **different**.

c) Janet works in an **accredited** laboratory. Circle the sentences about accreditation that are true.

- Accreditation shows that a lab meets internationally agreed standards of working.
- Accreditation shows that a lab cannot produce reliable results.
- Staff in an accredited lab are unable to work to a good level.
- Accredited labs can be trusted to carry out work in a standard way.

d) Janet's laboratory has been sent a water sample as part of a **proficiency test**.

i) What are proficiency tests used for?

....

....

ii) The graph shows the proficiency test results from five different labs. Janet works for lab B. Has her lab passed the proficiency test? Give a reason for your answer.

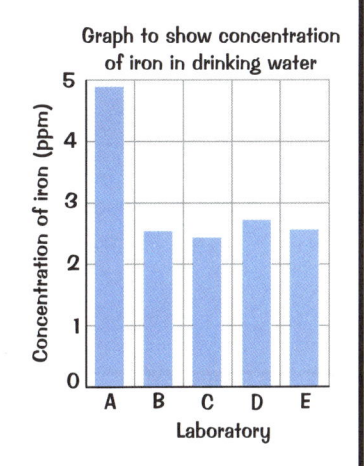

....

....

Module 3 — Scientific Detection

Visual Examination

Q1 Chantelle is a scientific officer for the **Environment Agency**. She specialises in dealing with the aftermath of **floods**.

a) When Chantelle arrives at the scene of a flood she starts by visually examining the area. Give **four** ways that Chantelle can record what she sees.

1. ....
2. ....
3. ....
4. ....

b) Chantelle needs to calculate the area affected when a lake floods. A helicopter takes aerial photographs of the area. Chantelle uses these photos and a grid map of the lake to make a diagram of the flood area. Her diagram is shown below.

Key
- ☐ Lake
- ▨ Flood area
- ☐ One square mile
- ⌂ Housing

i) Use the diagram to estimate the area covered by the lake.

.... square miles

ii) Calculate the area of the flood, including the lake. Use the equation, area of a circle = $\pi \times r^2$, where $\pi = 3.14$ and r = radius of the circle.

The radius is the distance from the centre of the circle to the edge.

....

.... square miles

iii) Use your answers from parts **i)** and **ii)** to calculate the area of the flood **not** including the lake.

.... square miles

Top Tips: For the exam, make sure you know how to calculate the **area** of shapes like rectangles and circles — and also make sure you've practised using a **linear scale**, such as a ruler.

Module 3 — Scientific Detection

Visual Examination

Q2 Police investigating the theft of a canal boat find some muddy **shoe prints** inside the boathouse where the boat was kept. **Photograph A** below shows the shoe print left at the scene of the theft. **Photographs B**, **C** and **D** show prints obtained in the **forensic laboratory** from the shoes of the **boat owner** (B) and **two suspects** (C and D).

a) Suggest **two** features of the shoe prints that the forensic scientists might compare.

1. ....

2. ....

b) i) Use the scale at the bottom of each photograph to estimate how **wide** (in cm) the shoe prints in **Photograph A** and **Photograph D** are at the widest point.

A ....

D ....

ii) Give **one** reason why the shoe that made the print shown in **Photograph D** couldn't have left the print at the crime scene.

....

c) Do any of the shoe prints match the one found at the crime scene? Give a reason for your answer.

....

....

Top Tips: When making visual examinations remember to look for both **similarities** and **differences** between the evidence — look at the size, shape, colour and any distinctive marks. Easy.

Module 3 — Scientific Detection

Light Microscopes

Q1 Mohammad works for the local council as a **public analyst**. He inspects food service companies and monitors their **food hygiene practices**. He often takes samples from the food preparation areas to inspect under a **light microscope**.

a) Label the picture of a light microscope. Two parts have been done for you.

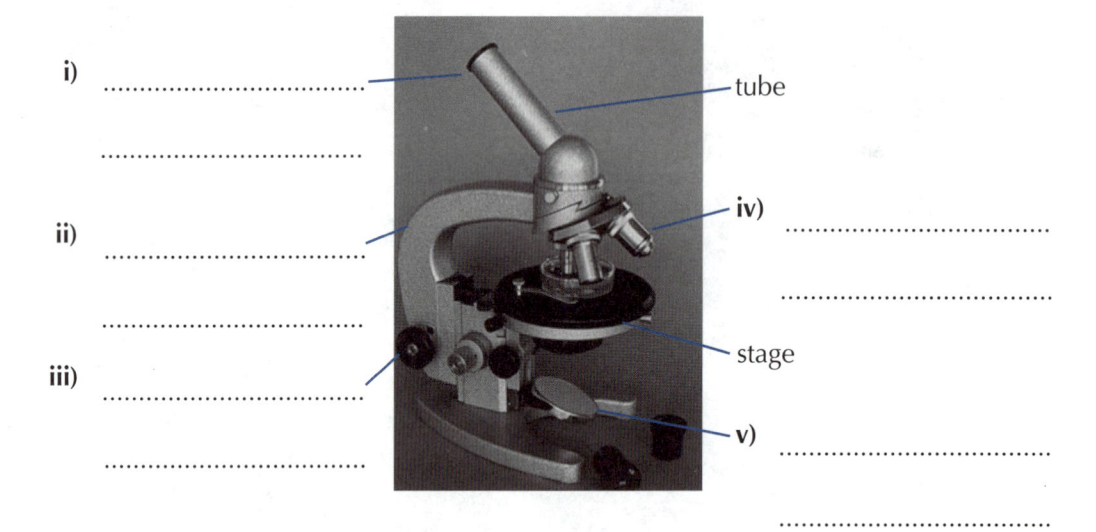

i) ....
....
ii) ....
iii) ....
....

tube
iv) ....
....
stage
v) ....
....

b) Draw lines to match the parts labelled above to their purpose.

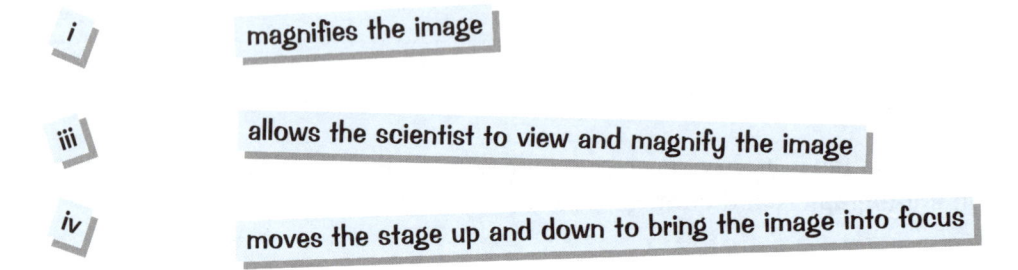

i — magnifies the image

iii — allows the scientist to view and magnify the image

iv — moves the stage up and down to bring the image into focus

c) Circle the correct word in each pair to complete the paragraph below.

Microscopes use mirrors / **lenses** to magnify images. This makes them look smaller / **bigger**. Microscopes also **increase** / decrease the resolution of an image. This **increases** / decreases the detail you can see.

d) Calculate the magnifying power of Mohammad's microscope.
His eyepiece lens has a magnification of ×10 and his objective lens has a magnification of ×40.

....

Module 3 — Scientific Detection

Light Microscopes

Q2 A **forensic scientist** is preparing a temporary **slide** of a hair sample found at the scene of a crime.

a) i) Number the statements below (1-5) to show the correct method for preparing a light microscope slide.

☐ Gently place the cover slip over the sample.

☐ Add any required stain to the sample.

☐ Place the sample on the slide.

☐ Tap with a needle to remove any air bubbles.

☐ Add some mountant to the slide.

ii) Why is a mountant added to the slide?

....

b) The picture below shows the hair sample found at the **crime scene** under a light microscope.

Reference Samples
— Blonde hair
— Brown hair
— Chemically damaged hair
— Undamaged hair

i) What is the diameter of the hair at point X?

....

Use the scale on the pictures to measure the diameter.

ii) Other than diameter, give **two** features of the hair.

....

....

iii) The hair sample to the right belongs to a **suspect**. Does the sample taken from the suspect match that found at the crime scene? Give a reason for your answer.

....

....

Module 3 — Scientific Detection

Light Microscopes

Q3 Residents of a town have complained of stomach upsets, possibly caused by contaminated **drinking water**. The water company that supplies the town takes water from a reservoir, **treats** it and stores it in tanks. A scientist collects water **samples** from the reservoir (**A**) and tanks (**B**) to check for **bacteria** that may cause illness.

The picture shows the stained samples under a light microscope. The bacteria have been labelled and a key has been included to help with your descriptions.

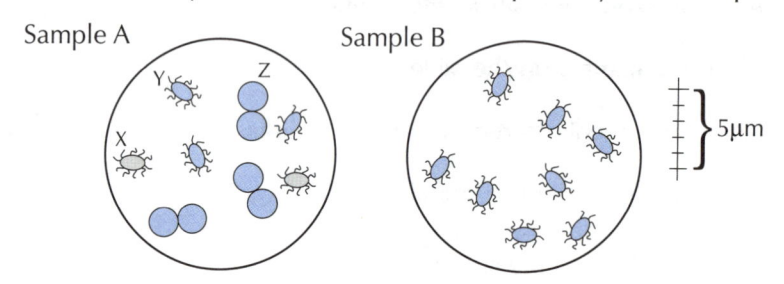

Sample A   Sample B

}5μm

Reference Sample

- ⊙⊙ Negative staining diplococci
- ⊙⊙ Positive staining diplococci
- Negative staining bacilli with flagella
- Positive staining bacilli with flagella

a) Use the reference samples to identify the three types of bacteria.

X ....

Y ....

Z ....

b) Complete the table below by counting and measuring the main features in each sample.

Bacteria	Number in Sample A	Number in Sample B	Width (μm)
X	2		
Y			
Z			

Josie was shocked to see a Diplodocus under the microscope

c) One type of negative staining diplococci is known to commonly cause stomach upsets. Is it likely that the residents' stomach upsets have been caused by this negative staining diplococci? Give a reason for your answer.

....

....

Module 3 — Scientific Detection

Electron Microscopes

Q1 In an **electron microscope**, a beam of **electrons** is fired at the sample. Electrons are part of **atoms**.

a) Draw lines to link the part of an atom with its charge.

Electrons   Positive

Nucleus   Negative

b) Label this diagram of an atom.

i) ....

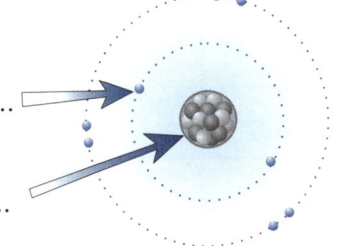

ii) ....

Q2 The getaway car used in a **bank robbery** hit a **bollard** in the road as it sped away from the crime scene. Forensic scientists collected **flecks of paint** to examine using an **electron microscope**.

a) Complete the following passage using the words below.

| electrons | freezing | metal | micrograph | thin | vacuum |

Before viewing a sample under an electron microscope it has to be processed, e.g. by .... it or coating it in .... The sample is cut into .... sections and placed under an electron microscope. The image produced is called an electron ....

b) Why did the forensic scientists use an electron microscope instead of a light microscope? Tick the correct answer.

Electron microscopes can see colour, light microscopes can't. ☐

Electron microscopes can show greater detail than light microscopes, due to a greater magnification. ☐

Sample preparation is easier for an electron microscope than it is for a light microscope. ☐

c) Are electron microscopes more or less **expensive** than light microscopes?

....

Module 3 — Scientific Detection

Electron Microscopes

Q3 The police have found a dead body in a park. The autopsy found that the man has **water** in his lungs, which indicates he **drowned**. The pathologist collects a sample of the water for analysis. Forensic scientists can estimate where a person drowned by looking at the number and type of different **diatoms** (types of algae) in the water. The diatom composition is unique.

The electron micrograph of the diatoms found in a small volume of the water sample is shown on the right.

a) Complete the table about the main features of the electron micrograph.

Diatom	Number in sample	Diameter (µm)
X		
Y		
Z		

Here are some reference diagrams of diatoms.

Eupodiscus species

Paralia species

Campylosira species

Auliscus species

Arachnoidiscus species

Cyclotella species

b) Use the reference diagrams to identify the diatoms found in the water sample from the man's lungs.

X ....

Y ....

Z ....

The forensic scientist collects water samples from three different rivers in the area. The table on the right shows the diatoms found in each sample.

c) Which river might the man have drowned in?

....

River	Diatoms present
1	*Auliscus* species *Arachnoidiscus* species *Paralia* species
2	*Paralia* species *Auliscus* species *Eupodiscus* species
3	*Camplylosira* species *Cyclotella* species *Arachnoidiscus* species

Top Tips: Interpreting electron micrographs is the same as interpreting images from light microscopes — **describe**, **count**, **measure** and **identify** the main features.

Module 3 — Scientific Detection

Chromatography

Q1 The **Environment Agency** are tracing the source of **pollution** in a river. They use paper **chromatography** to help them analyse the pollution.

a) Number the following statements (1-5) to show the correct method for carrying out paper chromatography.

- [ ] Compare the results to reference materials.
- [ ] Draw a line across the bottom of a piece of filter paper.
- [ ] Allow time for the solvent to seep up the paper.
- [ ] Place spots of the samples to be tested at regular intervals along the line.
- [ ] Hang the sheet in a beaker of solvent.

b) Complete the following passage using words from the list below, to describe how paper chromatography works.

different   more   dissolve   stationary   mobile   faster
             solvent

In paper chromatography, substances are separated by the movement of a solvent (known as the .... phase) through a medium (known as the .... phase). The solvent rises up the filter paper and when it reaches the spots of sample, the chemicals in the sample .... The solvent carries the different chemicals in the sample up the filter paper at .... rates. The more soluble the chemical, the .... time it spends in the mobile phase and so the .... it travels up the paper.

Q2 Gerald wants to compare the ink used to make **forged banknotes** with some ink found at a suspect's house. He's trying to decide whether to use paper, thin layer or gas **chromatography**.

a) What is the main **difference** between thin layer chromatography and paper chromatography?

....

....

b) What **advantages** does gas chromatography have compared to paper chromatography and thin layer chromatography? Circle the **three** correct answers.

It produces quantitative data from small samples.   It uses standard reference samples.   It has a greater separating power.   Its cheaper.   It can be used to separate gases, liquids or volatile solids.

Module 3 — Scientific Detection

Chromatography

Q3 Ella is using **paper chromatography** to compare the **ink** used on a **threatening letter** with the ink found in three **suspects' printers**.

a) Circle the correct word in each pair to complete the sentence below.

The **solvent** / **gas** used in paper chromatography depends on the **solvent** / **sample** being tested. Some compounds dissolve well in water but others are more soluble in **non-aqueous** / **aqueous** solvents.

b) When Ella analyses the ink from the threatening letter and the ink from the suspects' printers she obtains the chromatogram shown on the right.

Suggest which ink could have been used to produce the letter.

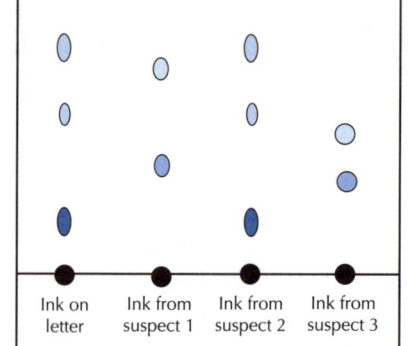

....

Q4 A scientist at the **Food Standards Agency** is testing some foods for banned **food colourings** using paper chromatography. She compares the results from three fruit juices with **reference samples** for two banned food colourings.

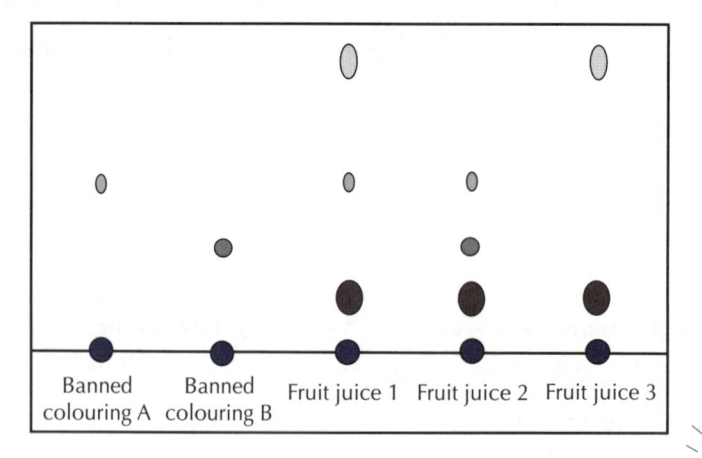

Tick the boxes below to show which colouring, if any, each of the fruit juices contains.

Compare the spots contained in the colourings and the juices.

	contains colouring A	contains colouring B	contains neither
Fruit juice 1	☐	☐	☐
Fruit juice 2	☐	☐	☐
Fruit juice 3	☐	☐	☐

Module 3 — Scientific Detection

Electrophoresis

Q1 **DNA profiling** is an important tool, widely used by forensic scientists to link a suspect to a crime scene.

a) Complete the passage about DNA profiling using words from the list below.

> unique   identical twins   electrophoresis   DNA   small

DNA profiling uses .... to compare ....
fragments. It's useful because everyone's DNA is .... (except
..................................). Comparisons with known fragments can help to
identify unknown fragments. DNA can be extracted from ....
biological samples.

b) Give **two** samples that scientists might collect from a crime scene that contain DNA.

1. ....   2. ....

c) Other than linking a suspect to a crime scene, give **two** examples of uses for DNA profiling.

1. ....

2. ....

DNA profiling isn't only used in forensics.

Q2 The **Food Standards Agency** is investigating the claim that a caviar manufacturer is selling cheap (salmon or whitefish) caviar as expensive (beluga) caviar.
They compare the **DNA profile** from two random samples of caviar taken from the manufacturer to reference DNA profiles from salmon, beluga and whitefish caviar.

Reference Profiles: Salmon, Beluga, Whitefish, Sample 1, Sample 2

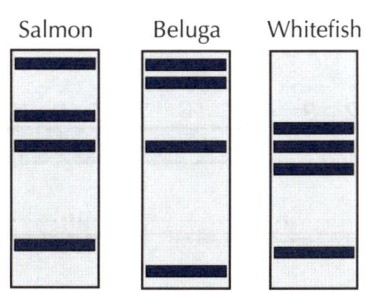

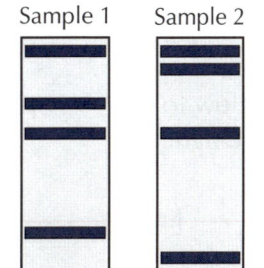

Compare the bands from the reference samples with those from the caviar samples.

What conclusions can be drawn from these results?

....

....

Top Tips: The reason DNA profiling is so useful in forensics is because DNA is unique (with the exception of identical twins) — there's no one else out there with the same DNA. Plus criminals are always leaving hair, skin cells and even the odd bit of blood at the scenes of crimes.

Module 3 — Scientific Detection

Colour Matching

Q1 Alisha is using **litmus paper** to test the **acidity** of some **orange juice**.

a) Circle the correct word in each pair to complete the sentences about litmus paper.

   i) Blue litmus paper turns red in alkalis / acids.

   ii) Red litmus paper turns blue in alkalis / acids.

b) What kind of test is the litmus test? Circle the correct answer.

   Qualitative   Semi-quantitative   Quantitative

Q2 James is investigating claims that a food manufacturer has been using an **illegal food additive**. He knows the illegal additive is **alkaline** and all other additives of this type have a **neutral pH**.

a) i) Name a solution, other than litmus, that James could use to test the pH of the additives.

   ....

   ii) What kind of results are produced by the test you named in i)? Circle the correct answer.

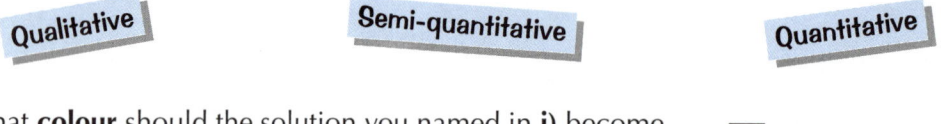

   Qualitative   Semi-quantitative   Quantitative

   iii) What **colour** should the solution you named in i) become when added to the illegal additive? Tick the correct box.

   ☐ Yellow
   ☐ Purple
   ☐ Red

b) James adds a few drops of a pH testing solution to samples of the four different additives used at the factory. The pH scale for the solution used is shown below.

   i) Use the words given below to complete the pH scale diagram.

   Neutral   Alkalis   Acids

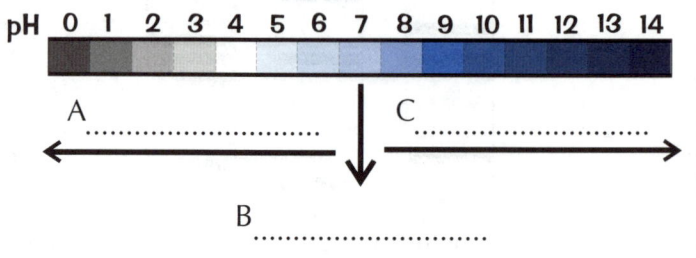

   pH 0 1 2 3 4 5 6 7 8 9 10 11 12 13 14

   A ....   C ....

   B ....

   ii) The results of James's tests are shown on the right. Which of the samples could be the illegal additive?

   ....

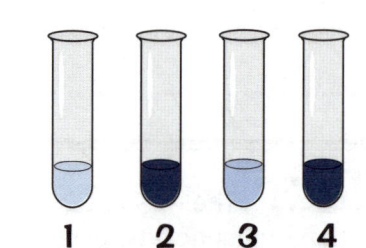

   1   2   3   4

Module 3 — Scientific Detection

Colour Matching

Q3 Gwen is constantly thirsty and suffers from blurred vision. Her doctor thinks she may have **diabetes**. The doctor can use a **colour test kit** to give a preliminary diagnosis.

a) What is the name of the colour test kit Gwen's doctor will use?

....

b) What does the test carried out by Gwen's doctor detect? Circle the correct answer.

Glucose in urine   **Glucose in the liver**

Protein in urine   **Protein in the blood**

c) Gwen's test result is shown below on the left and the key to the result is shown below on the right.

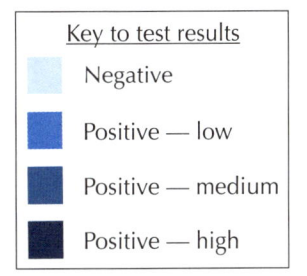

Key to test results
- Negative
- Positive — low
- Positive — medium
- Positive — high

Does the result of the test indicate that Gwen might have diabetes? Explain your answer.

....

Q4 Asma thinks she's **pregnant**. She buys a pregnancy test kit from her local pharmacy.

a) What do pregnancy test kits detect? Circle the correct answer.

Glucose in urine   **Glucose in the blood**

A hormone (HCG) in urine   **A hormone (HCG) in saliva**

b) Asma's test result is shown on the left and the key to the result is shown on the right.

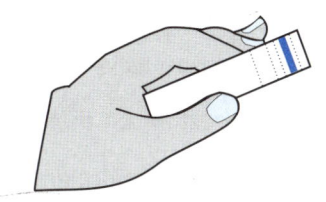

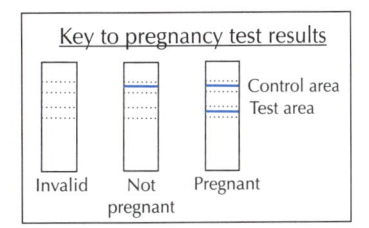

Key to pregnancy test results

Control area
Test area

Invalid   Not pregnant   Pregnant

Does the result of the test indicate that Asma is pregnant?

....

Module 3 — Scientific Detection

Colorimetry

Q1 Colorimetry can be used to calculate the concentration of chemicals.

a) What does a colorimeter measure?

....

b) Circle the correct word(s) to complete the sentences below.

i) Colorimetry is **cheaper** / **more expensive** than colour matching and is usually **faster** / **slower**.

ii) Colorimetry needs to be performed in a **fume cupboard** / **laboratory**.

c) What type of result does colorimetry produce? Tick the correct answer.

Qualitative ☐

Semi-quantitative ☐

Quantitative ☐

d) Before taking any measurements colorimeters must be set to zero. Describe how this is done.

....

Q2 Christopher is measuring the amount of carbohydrate in a drink to make sure the product is **labelled correctly**. He uses a chemical that turns blue when carbohydrate is present. The **more** carbohydrate, the deeper the shade of **blue**. Christopher uses **colorimetry** to measure the colour.

Christopher measures the absorbance of some reference samples of known carbohydrate concentration. His results are given below.

Carbohydrate concentration (g/ml)	Absorbance (absorbance units)
0.2	0.25
0.4	0.40
0.6	0.60
0.8	0.75
1.0	1.0

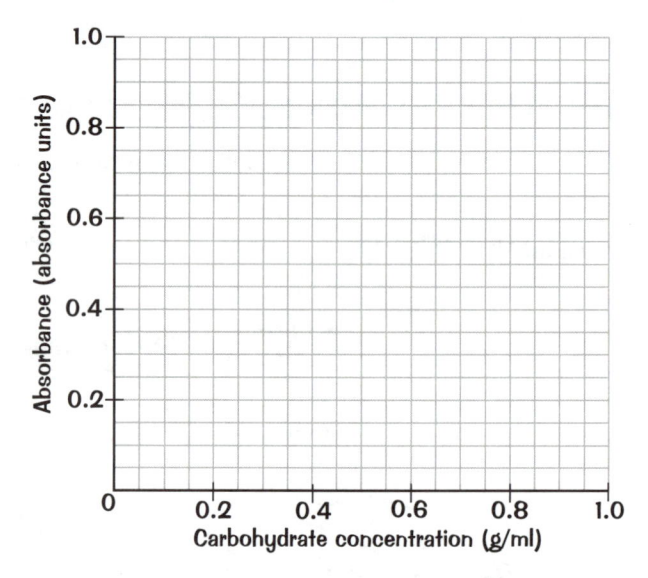

a) Use Christopher's results to draw a calibration graph, with a line of best fit, on the axes above.

b) The absorbance of an unknown drink sample is **0.55** absorbance units. Use the graph to work out the concentration of carbohydrate in the unknown sample. Show your working on the graph.

....

Module 3 — Scientific Detection

Scientific Evidence

Q1 Abdul is a **crime scene investigator**. He has gone to the scene of a murder to **collect evidence**.

Complete the following passage using the words below.

contamination   representative   sealed   protective   deteriorating

When collecting evidence from the crime scene, Abdul should make sure he collects .... samples. He can help prevent the evidence from .... by storing it properly. He should wear .... clothing to avoid .... of the evidence. Any samples collected should be stored in .... bags or containers to avoid any tampering.

Q2 Alvina is following a **standard procedure** to determine the concentration of iron in a sample of drinking water using colorimetry.

a) Suggest **two** reasons why Alvina uses standard procedure to carry out her work.

1. ....

2. ....

Think about Alvina's results.

b) Alvina **calibrates** the colorimeter before each use. Suggest a reason why.

....

c) Alvina has three water samples, A, B and C. She tests each one three times and then calculates an average concentration for each sample. Complete the table below by calculating the average iron concentration of each sample. Sample A has been done for you.

Sample	Concentration (parts per million)			
	1	2	3	Average
A	0.12	0.13	0.11	0.12
B	0.21	0.19	0.21	
C	0.25	0.22	0.23	

Top Tips: It's really important to **collect**, **store** and **prepare** samples for analysis correctly. If someone has used standard procedures when carrying out their experiments and investigations, it's the first sign that you can trust their data — they're safe, effective and accurate methods.

Module 3 — Scientific Detection

Scientific Evidence

Q3 Rose works for the **Food Standards Agency**. She has received a tip-off that some crisps have **fewer grams** per packet than stated on the **label**. She tests three brands by weighing the amount of crisps in four packets of each brand and calculating an average.

a) Rose uses a top-pan balance that has to be calibrated before use.
Number the statements (1-3) to show how Rose will calibrate the top-pan balance.

- [ ] The sample to be tested is placed on the balance
- [ ] The balance is adjusted to show the correct mass of the reference sample
- [ ] A reference sample of known mass is placed on the balance

Rose measures the mass of crisps found in each packet.
She adds the information to the table shown below.

Brand	Mass per packet (g)				
	1	2	3	4	Average
A	45	44	44	46	44.8
B	36	38	38	37	
C	37	48	48	47	

When calculating an average, remember not to include any outliers.

b) Identify any **outliers** in the data.

....

c) i) Complete the table by calculating the average mass of crisps. Brand A has been done for you.

ii) Draw a bar chart showing the average mass per packet (g) for each brand using the axes below. Brand A has been done for you.

Bar chart to show the average mass of crisps per packet for brands A, B and C

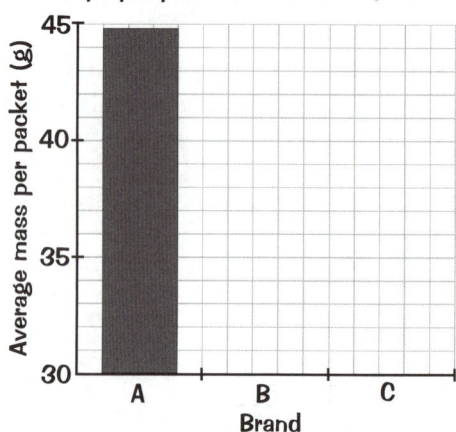

iii) All three brands were labelled as containing **45 g** of crisps per packet.
What conclusions can you draw from the data?

....

....

Module 3 — Scientific Detection

Mixed Questions for Module 3

Q1 Police are investigating the **shooting** of a young man. A **bullet** collected from the crime scene and a **blood sample** collected from the jumper of a suspect have been sent away for **forensic analysis**.

The bullet used in the shooting is examined using a light microscope.

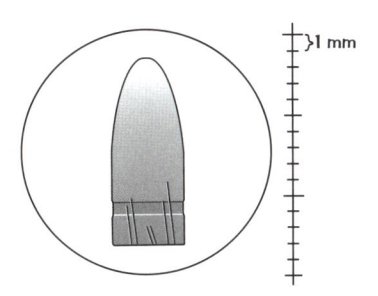

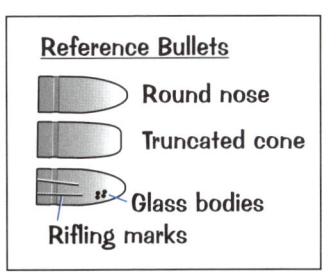

Reference Bullets
- Round nose
- Truncated cone
- Glass bodies
- Rifling marks

a) Describe the main features of the bullet using the reference bullets to help.

....

b) Measure the width of the bullet at it's widest point.

....

c) The picture on the right shows a bullet fired from the gun of a suspect.

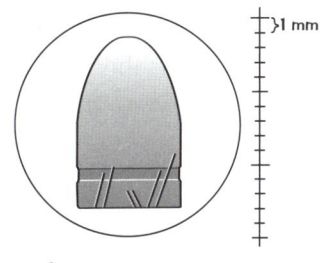

   i) List one **similarity** between the bullet from the suspect's gun and the bullet retrieved from the crime scene.

   ....

   ii) Do you think the suspect's gun was used in the shooting? Give a reason for your answer.

   ....
   ....

d) The microscope used to examine the bullets has an objective lens magnification of **×10** and an eyepiece lens magnification of **×4**. Work out the magnifying power of the microscope.

....

e) The scientists use **DNA profiling** to compare the DNA from the blood found on the suspect's clothing with the DNA of the victim. The results are shown below.

   i) Name the technique used to produce the DNA profiles.

   ....

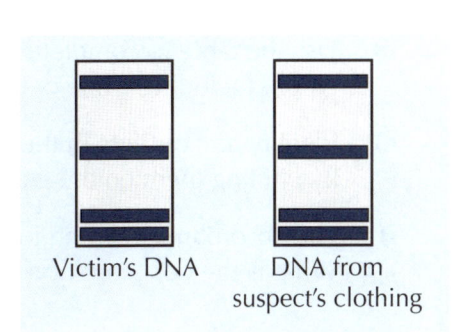

   ii) What conclusion can you draw from the DNA profiles?

   ....
   ....

Victim's DNA   DNA from suspect's clothing

Module 3 — Scientific Detection

Mixed Questions for Module 3

Q2 The Environment Agency has sent out a scientist to investigate a ship that is spilling **toxic chemicals** into the sea.

a) The diagram shows the area of the chemical spill. Calculate the area of the chemical spill.

.... square km

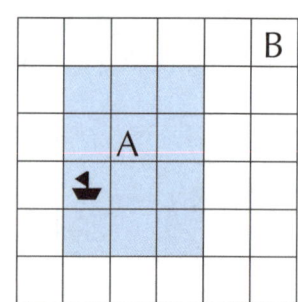

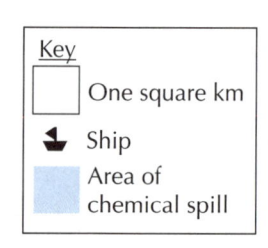

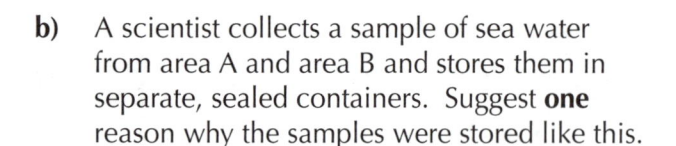

b) A scientist collects a sample of sea water from area A and area B and stores them in separate, sealed containers. Suggest **one** reason why the samples were stored like this.

....

c) The scientist measures the pH of the samples using universal indicator solution. The results and the pH scale used are given below.

i) What is the pH of each sample?

A ....

B ....

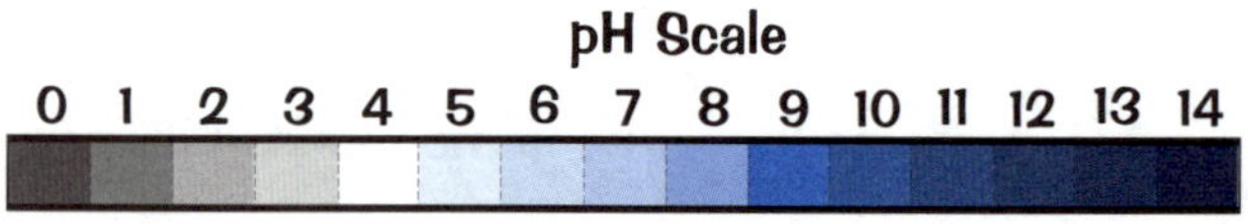

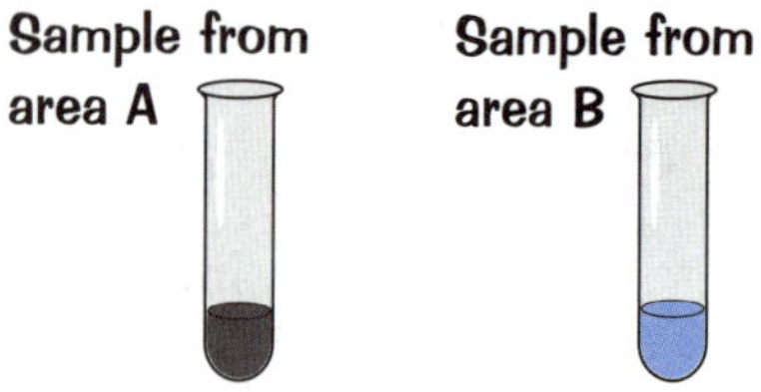

ii) Is the sample taken from the area of the chemical spill acid or alkaline?

....

The scientist uses **colorimetry** to determine the **concentration** of the chemical in Sample A. A solution is used that will turn **red** if the chemical is present. The **more** chemical present the **deeper** the shade of red. The absorbance readings from reference samples of known concentrations are given in the table below.

Concentration (parts per million)	Absorbance (absorbance units)
10	0.60
20	0.75
30	0.80
40	0.90
50	1.0

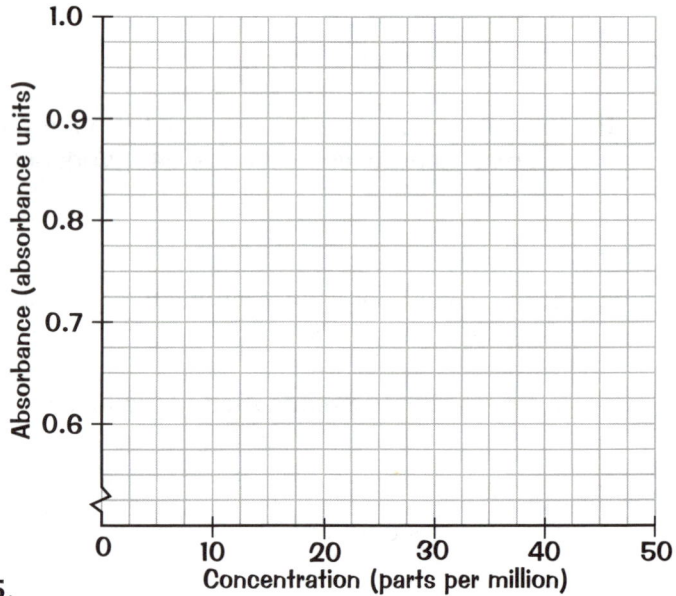

d) Use the table to complete the calibration graph, including a line of best fit.

e) Identify any **outliers** in the data by circling them on the graph.

f) The absorbance reading for sample A is **0.85**. What is the concentration of the chemical in Sample A?

....

Module 4 — Harnessing Chemicals

Chemistry and Symbols

Q1 Robert works in a **chemistry laboratory** as a lab assistant. He has been asked to collect some elements from the store cupboard.

a) Write the **names** of the **elements** he needs to collect.

K ....

Ca ....

Zn ....

S ....

Na ....

These are just a few of the eleven elements you need to know. Make sure you know both the symbol and the chemical name.

b) Robert also finds the **compounds** shown below.
Use the formulas on the labels below to answer the following questions.

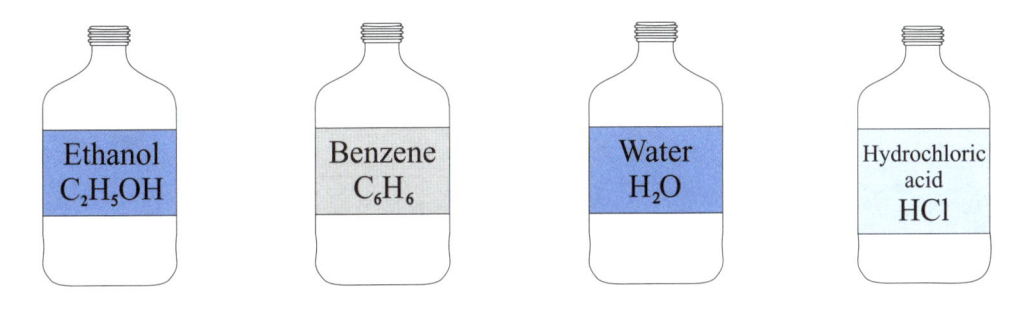

Ethanol C_2H_5OH Benzene C_6H_6 Water H_2O Hydrochloric acid HCl

i) How many oxygen atoms are there in one molecule of ethanol? ....

ii) How many carbon atoms are there in one molecule of benzene? ....

iii) How many hydrogen atoms are there in one molecule of water? ....

iv) How many chlorine atoms are there in one molecule of hydrochloric acid? ....

v) How many hydrogen atoms are there in one molecule of ethanol? ....

c) Robert finds a bottle which displays a symbol indicating that the contents are toxic.
What does **toxic** mean?

....

Top Tips: There are eleven elements you need to be able to recall, with their symbols. Most of the symbols are pretty straightforward, like Mg for Magnesium. There are a few slightly tricky ones, like Cl and Ca, so think carefully. The symbol for sodium is just a bit weird — makes no sense to me.

Chemistry and Symbols

Q2 Nadim works in a **hospital**. He comes across many different types of chemicals, some of them **hazardous**. Fill in the meaning of each hazard symbol below by choosing the correct label from the box.

> corrosive   toxic   irritant
>
> harmful   highly flammable   oxidising

a) ....

b) ....

c) ....

d) ....

e) ....

f) ....

Q3 A student is looking at the **labels** on the **chemicals** in the school laboratory.

a) Some of the chemicals are labelled as being **corrosive**.
What would happen if one of these was spilt on a person's hands?

....

b) Other chemicals are labelled as being **oxidising**.
Explain how they could be dangerous.

....

Top Tips: It's pretty important to understand hazard symbols — not only to pass your exam but also to make sure that you work safely in the lab when you're doing your own experiments.

Module 4 — Harnessing Chemicals

Laboratory Equipment

Q1 In a **cosmetic research laboratory**, a team of chemists is trying to formulate a new mascara.

The chemists use the following equipment.

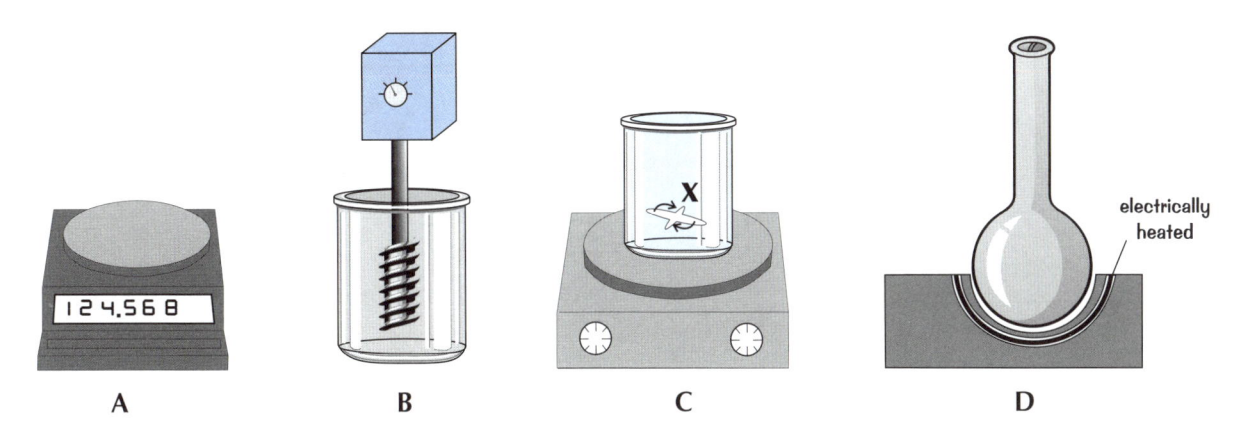

A   B   C   D

a) Draw a line to match each label from the pictures above with its correct name.

A — heating mantle

B — magnetic stirrer

C — balance

D — immersion heater

b) Give the name of object **X**, shown in diagram C above.

....

c) John, a chemist in the lab, is carrying out an experiment.
Complete the passage below using the words given.

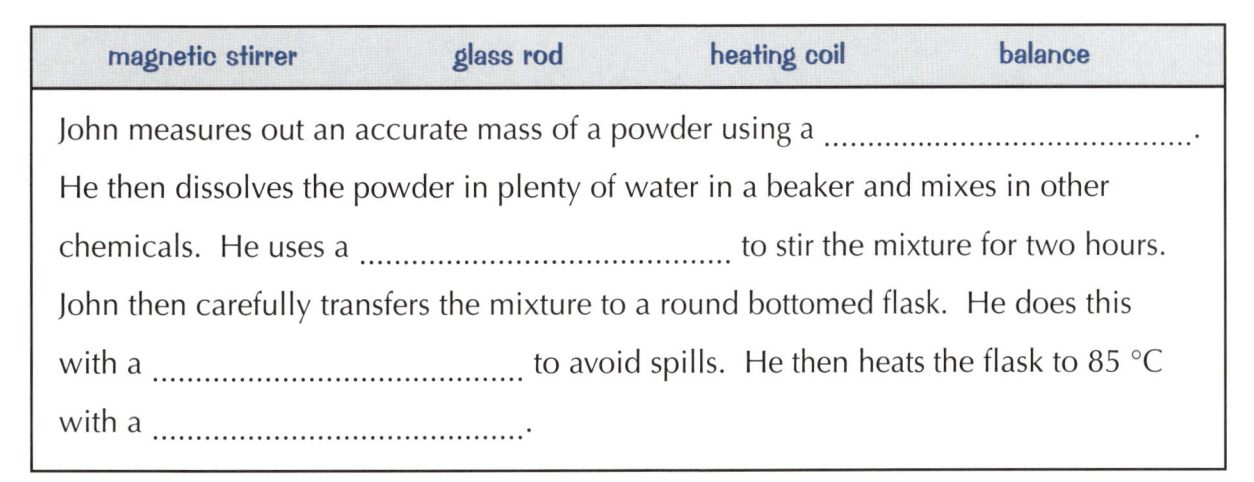

| magnetic stirrer | glass rod | heating coil | balance |

John measures out an accurate mass of a powder using a ....

He then dissolves the powder in plenty of water in a beaker and mixes in other

chemicals. He uses a .... to stir the mixture for two hours.

John then carefully transfers the mixture to a round bottomed flask. He does this

with a .... to avoid spills. He then heats the flask to 85 °C

with a ....

Module 4 — Harnessing Chemicals

Laboratory Equipment

Q2 Sarah is carrying out a **titration**.

a) Name the pieces of equipment labelled A, B and C.

A ....

B ....

C ....

b) Describe the function of **A**.

....

c) Sarah has a wide variety of equipment in her lab to help her carry out titrations.
Choose from the pieces of apparatus named below to answer the following questions.

Heating Mantle   **Tripod**   **Funnel**   **Pipette and Filler**   **Thermometer**

i) Sarah needs to add an **accurately measured volume** of liquid to a flask.
Which piece of equipment should she use?

....

ii) Before analysis, Sarah needs to **heat** a sample.
Which piece of equipment should she use?

....

iii) Sarah needs to **transfer** a powder from one container to another.
Which piece of equipment should she use?

....

Module 4 — Harnessing Chemicals

Acids and Alkalis

Q1 Frank is a **food scientist** who works for a drinks manufacturer.

a) i) Frank needs to know the **approximate pH** of a fizzy drink. What could he use to estimate this?

....

ii) Frank is asked to accurately test the pH of another fizzy drink, without using any chemicals. Suggest a way he could do this.

....

b) Frank was asked to test the pH of a fizzy drink and some other liquids. Tick the boxes to show whether the liquids he tested are acidic, alkaline or neutral.

	acidic	neutral	alkaline
i) Cola — pH 2.5	☐	☐	☐
ii) Pure water — pH 7	☐	☐	☐
iii) Beer — pH 4.5	☐	☐	☐

Q2 When pollutants enter a **lake** or **river** in large amounts they can alter the pH of the water.

Complete the passage below using the words provided, to describe how a change in the pH of a polluted lake could be reversed.

raise	acid	alkali	neutralisation
acidic		lower	oxidation

If a water sample taken from a lake is too ....,
then alkali needs be added to .... the pH.
However if the water sample is too alkaline then it is necessary to add
.... to the lake. This process is
called ....

Top Tips: Acids aren't just the bottles of stuff that chemists keep in their store rooms, that can burn your face off. Loads of things in the real world are acidic — like lemon juice. And wine.

Module 4 — Harnessing Chemicals

Acids and Alkalis

Q3 Simon is using **acids** and **alkalis** to make **salts**.

a) Complete the general word equation for **neutralisation**.

.... + ... → salt + ...

b) Simon uses several different acids.
Draw lines to match each acid with its correct formula.

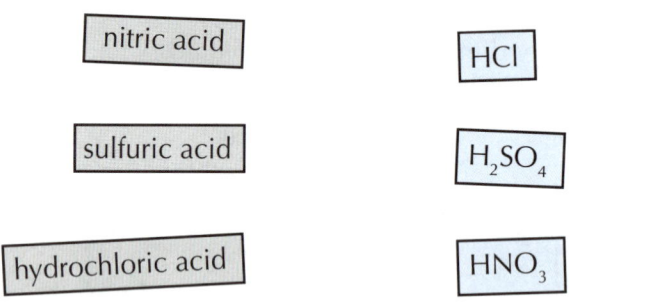

nitric acid   HCl

sulfuric acid H_2SO_4

hydrochloric acid HNO_3

c) Complete the following equations by choosing from the chemicals below.

| strontium hydroxide | water | lithium hydroxide |
| potassium sulfate | sodium nitrate | sulfuric acid |

i) hydrochloric acid + calcium hydroxide → calcium chloride + ...

ii) nitric acid + sodium hydroxide → .... + water

iii) .... + magnesium oxide → magnesium sulfate + water

iv) sulfuric acid + potassium hydroxide → .... + water

v) hydrochloric acid + ... → strontium chloride + water

vi) nitric acid + ... → lithium nitrate + water

Module 4 — Harnessing Chemicals

Reactions of Acids

Q1 A research scientist is developing a product to remove deposits of calcium carbonate (limescale) from kettles. She thinks that one way to get rid of it is to use a dilute acid. She tests this idea using nitric acid, sulfuric acid and hydrochloric acid.

Complete the word equations below to show the products that will be formed in these tests.

a) nitric acid + calcium carbonate

→ .... + ... + ...

b) sulfuric acid + calcium carbonate

→ .... + ... + ...

c) hydrochloric acid + calcium carbonate

→ .... + ... + ...

Q2 Gita adds a small piece of zinc to a test tube containing sulfuric acid.

a) Describe what Gita will see.

....

b) Write a word equation for the reaction between zinc and sulfuric acid.

....

Q3 James is investigating some chemicals that are used as food additives.

a) First, James investigates magnesium chloride. Name the metal and acid that can be used to produce magnesium chloride.

Metal: .... Acid: ....

b) James then researches aluminium sulfate. Write a word equation to show how aluminium sulfate could be prepared using a metal and an acid.

....

Top Tips: This page might just seem like a load of equations, but make sure you have a go at them all. You'll be glad of the practice when it comes to the exam — it's pretty likely that you'll be asked to write at least one equation. They're not too bad once you've got the hang of them. Honest.

Module 4 — Harnessing Chemicals

Solutions

Q1 A teacher is making **sodium hydroxide solution** of a known **concentration** for an experiment. The instructions she is following include the terms **solute**, **solvent** and **solution**.

Draw lines to match up each of these terms with the correct example on the right.

solute	sodium hydroxide
solvent	water
solution	sodium hydroxide dissolved in water

Q2 Albert is making up **stock solutions** in his lab.

A stock solution is just a large volume of a chemical at a known concentration.

a) Albert dissolved **50 g** of lithium chloride in water to make **250 cm³** of solution. What is the **concentration**, in g/litre, of the lithium chloride solution he has made?

....

....

b) Albert then dissolved **40 g** of copper sulfate in water to make **2 litres** of solution. What is the **concentration**, in g/litre, of the copper sulfate solution he has made up?

....

....

c) Albert wants to make a **75 g/litre** solution of sodium hydroxide. What **mass** of sodium hydroxide pellets should Albert dissolve to make **20 litres** of solution?

....

....

Q3 Clive's job is to make up **solutions** to sell to laboratories and factories. He has been asked to make up an order of **4 litres of 50 g/litre copper chloride** solution.

a) Before handling the copper chloride, what should Clive do?

....

b) Describe the steps Clive should take to make up this order.

....

....

....

Module 4 — Harnessing Chemicals

Solutions

Q4 It's George's job to make the chemical **solutions** for the science teachers in a school lab.

   a) His first job is to make up 3 litres of sodium chloride solution with a concentration of 10 g/litre.

   i) How much sodium chloride will it take to make up one litre of solution?

   ....

   ii) Using your answer to part i), how much sodium chloride does George need to make up 3 litres of solution?

   ....

   b) His next job is to make up 250 cm^3 of magnesium sulfate solution at a concentration of 8 g/litre. How much magnesium sulfate will it take to make up 250 cm^3 of solution?

   ....

   ....

   c) The next teacher specified his order slightly differently. He wanted 2 litres of copper chloride solution at a concentration of 0.25 g/cm^3. How much copper chloride will it take to make up 2 litres of solution?

   Remember: 1 litre = 1000 cm^3

   ....

   ....

Q5 A student evaporated a **200 cm^3** sample of sea water. He was left with 7 g of **sodium chloride**.

What was the concentration, in g/cm^3, of sodium chloride in the sea water?

....

....

Q6 Naveena is working out how much **solid** she needs to make various **solutions**.

   a) How many grams of magnesium chloride does she need to make 300 cm^3 of a 0.5 g/cm^3 solution?

   ....

   ....

   b) How many grams of sodium carbonate does she need to make 4 litres of a 50 g/litre solution?

   ....

   ....

Module 4 — Harnessing Chemicals

Making Insoluble Salts

Q1 Kamal is making some **insoluble salts** in his lab.

　a) Write **word** equations for the reactions that occur when he mixes:

　　i) lead nitrate solution and sodium iodide solution

　　..

　　ii) barium chloride solution and sodium sulfate solution

　　..

　　iii) silver nitrate solution and copper chloride solution

　　..

　b) Kamal carries out a reaction that produces soluble sodium nitrate and insoluble barium sulfate. Name the **two** chemicals that he reacted together.

　　..

Q2 Ghassan needs to make **copper hydroxide**, using the following reaction:

copper sulfate	+	sodium hydroxide	→	copper hydroxide	+	sodium sulfate
soluble		soluble		insoluble		soluble

　a) What will Ghassan see when he mixes the copper sulfate and sodium hydroxide solutions together?

　　..

　b) What is the name given to this type of reaction?

　　..

　c) Describe how Ghassan should **separate** the copper hydroxide from the solution.

　　..

　　..

　　..

　d) Why couldn't he use the same method to separate out sodium sulphate?

　　..

　　..

Module 4 — Harnessing Chemicals

Making Insoluble Salts

Q3 Keira is researching **lead iodide**, which can be used as a detector material for X-rays. She makes some **insoluble** lead iodide by mixing **lead nitrate** and **sodium iodide** and then **filters** the product and obtains a **filtrate** and a **residue**.

a) Write a word equation for the reaction used to make lead iodide.

....

b) What is meant by the term **filtrate**?

....

c) What is meant by the term **residue**?

....

d) After filtering the product, Keira rinses and dries the lead iodide.

   i) Why does the solid need to be rinsed?

   ....

   ii) Why is it important to use distilled water and not just tap water to rinse the solid?

   ....

   iii) Describe how the solid could be **dried** after rinsing.

   ....

Q4 Ron works for a company that makes insoluble chemicals. His job is to **save money** for the company and make their processes more **environmentally friendly**.

a) The company dries its products using drying ovens. Ron suggests that they could dry the products naturally in air. Give **two** reasons why Ron thinks this method would be environmentally better.

....

....

b) Suggest why the company might **not** implement Ron's idea.

....

....

Top Tips: It's important that you get the method for making insoluble salts straight in your mind. And that includes how to separate out your product at the end. It's pretty likely that you'll get asked something to do with these reactions, and those pesky word equations might show their faces.

Module 4 — Harnessing Chemicals

Making Soluble Salts

Q1 Magnesium sulfate can be used to increase the concentration of magnesium in soil. It is soluble and is made from magnesium oxide and sulfuric acid. Bob is making a sample of magnesium sulfate crystals.

a) Write a **word** equation for the reaction.

....

b) Use the words in the box to complete the passage below.

filtration	magnesium oxide	heating	acid	filtrate
distillation	stirring	sterilisation	residue	evaporation

Bob slowly adds the magnesium oxide powder to the acid, ...

the mixture as he does so. He knows that all the .... has

reacted when he sees bits of powder at the bottom of the beaker. Bob then gets rid of

the powder by .... Next, Bob removes the magnesium

sulfate from the .... by ....

c) Bob wants to make the magnesium sulfate crystals quite **quickly**.
The sentences below describe how he should do this, but they are in the wrong order.

Number the boxes to show the correct order.

☐ Put the solution in an evaporating basin.

☐ Scrape the residue out of the basin.

☐ Apply gentle heat with a Bunsen burner.

☐ Place the evaporating basin on a tripod and gauze.

Bob wanted the crystals quickly.

d) Describe how Bob could change his method if he wanted to produce **larger crystals**.

....

....

e) What **safety precautions** should be taken during this procedure?

....

....

Module 4 — Harnessing Chemicals

Making Soluble Salts

Q2 Janine wants to make an exact amount of **soluble copper chloride** by adding **insoluble copper oxide** to **hydrochloric acid**.

a) Write a **word** equation for this reaction.

....

b) Janine only needs to measure out **one** of the chemicals accurately.

i) Which chemical would she need to measure out accurately? Give a reason for your answer.

....

....

ii) Which **apparatus** would you suggest she used to measure out this chemical?

....

Q3 A chemistry class is reading through a method for making a **soluble salt**. They comes across the words **crystallisation**, **evaporation** and **residue**.

Draw lines to match each word with its correct description.

- crystallisation — the substance left in a container after another has been removed
- evaporation — the formation of solid particles from a solution
- residue — the conversion of water from a liquid to a gas

Q4 Bashira is making some **soluble salts** in the lab.

Write word equations for the reactions that occur when she mixes:

a) hydrochloric acid and sodium hydroxide

....

b) sulfuric acid and potassium hydroxide

....

Top Tips: You might not find making salts the most thrilling of topics, but it is important that you know about how to make and separate a soluble salt. You can't use the same techniques that you would for insoluble salts — so make sure you learn the different processes.

Module 4 — Harnessing Chemicals

Titrations

Q1 Sodium sulfate can be made by reacting sodium hydroxide (an alkali) with sulfuric acid.

sulfuric acid + sodium hydroxide → sodium sulfate + water

a) i) The alkali is added gradually to the acid. What happens to the pH of the reaction mixture as the alkali is added?

....

ii) The pH of the reaction mixture can be measured using a pH meter.
How else could the pH be measured?

....

b) Fill in the gaps to complete the sentence.

> When the pH reaches exactly .... the reaction is complete.
> The acid and alkali have .... each other.

c) Once the reaction is complete, how are crystals of sodium sulfate obtained from the solution?

....

Q2 Chemists often draw graphs to represent how the pH of a mixture changes during a titration. The graph below shows how the pH changes when sulfuric acid is added to sodium hydroxide solution.

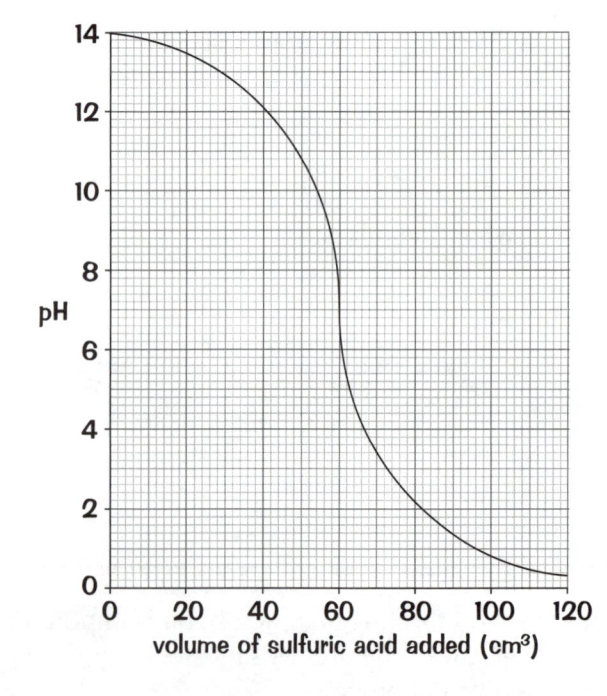

a) What was the pH of the sodium hydroxide solution **before** the titration?

....

b) How much sulfuric acid was needed to **neutralise** the alkali?

....

c) On the graph, sketch how the pH would change if alkali was being added to acid.

Module 4 — Harnessing Chemicals

Organic and Inorganic Chemicals

Q1 Chemicals can be obtained from **living**, **non-living** or **never lived** sources. Give two examples of **products** from each category.

a) Living:
....

b) Non-living:
....

c) Never lived:
....

Q2 A **garden chair** has its seat and back made from lightweight **plastic**.

a) What is the difference between organic and inorganic chemicals?
....
....

b) Explain why plastic is classed as an **organic** material.
....
....

c) The chair has **metal** legs. What type of material is metal?
Underline the correct answer.   organic   inorganic

Q3 Jimmy has made a table to show whether chemicals are **organic** or **inorganic**. Complete the table by saying whether each chemical is organic or inorganic.

Name	Formula	Organic or inorganic?
Benzene	C_6H_6	
Bromine	Br_2	
Propanone	C_3H_6O	
Silica	SiO_2	
Sulfuric acid	H_2SO_4	
Toluene	C_7H_8	
Zinc oxide	ZnO	

Don't worry if you don't know some of the chemicals — just look at what they contain.

that's organic

Module 4 — Harnessing Chemicals

Organic and Inorganic Chemicals

Q4 Indicate, by circling Y or N, which of the compounds in the table are **hydrocarbons**.

Formula	Hydrocarbon?
C_3H_8	Y / N
$C_3H_8O_2$	Y / N
C_3H_9N	Y / N
CCl_4	Y / N
HNO_3	Y / N
C_4H_8	Y / N
C_8H_{10}	Y / N
C_4H_8O	Y / N
C_3H_8O	Y / N

Q5 Many **shampoo manufacturers** add **salicylic acid** to their shampoo. It treats dandruff.

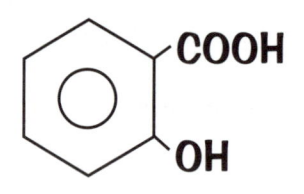

a) Is salicylic acid a **carboxylic acid**? ....

b) Give the two **functional groups** that salicylic acid contains.

....

Q6 Most **limestone** is formed from the remains of dead sea creatures that lived millions of years ago. Its chemical formula is **$CaCO_3$**.

a) Andy believes that limestone should be classed as **organic**. Suggest two reasons Andy might give for thinking this.

....

....

b) Some **sea water** contains dissolved limestone, which precipitates out when the water evaporates. Would you class limestone like this as organic or inorganic? Explain your answer.

....

....

Module 4 — Harnessing Chemicals

Making Esters

Q1 **Phenyl ethyl ethanoate** is a chemical used to provide a scent in some **perfumes**. It is manufactured from **phenyl ethanol** and **ethanoic acid**.

phenyl ethanol + ethanoic acid → phenyl ethyl ethanoate + water

....

a) Label the reaction above using the words in the box below.

| ester | alcohol | carboxylic acid |

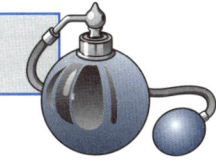

b) Explain why the reaction mixture is known as a **non-aqueous** solution.

....

c) The reaction takes place very slowly at room temperature. The mixture can be heated to speed up the reaction. Suggest one other thing that can be done to speed up the reaction.

....

d) A **condenser** is used to stop any vapours escaping from the flask during heating.

i) Explain how the condenser stops vapours escaping from the flask.

....

....

....

ii) What is this process known as?

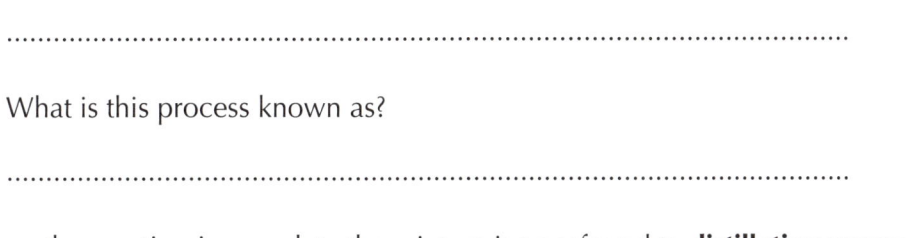

....

e) When the reaction is complete the mixture is transferred to **distillation apparatus**.

i) What is the purpose of distillation?

....

ii) What is the distilled liquid called?

....

Top Tips: This esters stuff can seem a bit tricky at first — there are a couple of processes to understand and a few fancy words in there. Stick at it though and you'll soon be doing it with your eyes closed. It's probably not advisable to close your eyes in the exam though.

Module 4 — Harnessing Chemicals

Mixtures

Q1 **Mayonnaise** is made by blending together vegetable oil and egg yolk to form an **emulsion**.

a) What is an emulsion?

....

b) What will happen to an emulsion of egg yolk and oil if it is left for a few days?

....

c) Explain why **emulsifiers** are added to emulsions.

....

d) Name two other household products that are emulsions.

....

....

Q2 Tick the boxes to show which of the sentences below are **true** or **false**.

	True	False
a) Emulsions are all edible.	☐	☐
b) Ice cream is an example of an emulsion.	☐	☐
c) Emulsions are always cloudy.	☐	☐
d) In an emulsion one component dissolves in another.	☐	☐

Q3 **Calamine lotion** is a popular treatment for skin irritation. It is a **suspension** of calamine powder in **water**.

a) What is a suspension?

....

b) Explain why a bottle of calamine lotion gets a clear layer on top if it's left standing for a few weeks.

....

c) Give another example of a suspension that you might find in the home.

....

Top Tips: Emulsions, mixtures and suspensions — another batch of technical words to add to your vocabulary. Luckily for you, there's some more practice with these on the next page...

Module 4 — Harnessing Chemicals

Mixtures

Q4 Harold creates a **suspension** in a jar by mixing silt with water. Complete the diagrams below by drawing **silt particles** to show the **suspension**, and also to show what will have happened inside the jar a **few hours later**.

Initial suspension   After a few hours

Q5 Before water has been added, **concrete** is a **mixture** of cement, sand and gravel.

a) What is a mixture?

....

b) The pie chart shows the composition of a concrete mixture. What is the percentage of **gravel** in this concrete powder? ....

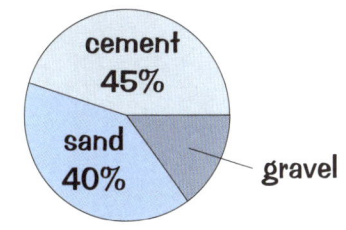

c) Name another common mixture of solids.

....

cement 45%
sand 40%
gravel

d) Kevin is testing concrete mixtures to see which is the **strongest**. He sets up the apparatus as shown in the diagram below.

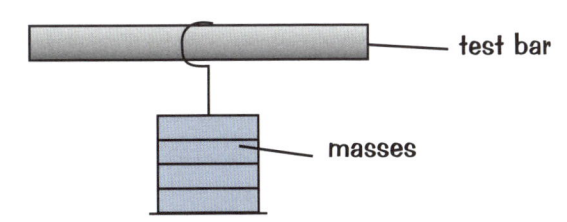

— test bar
— masses

Complete Kevin's results table.

	% of composition A	% of composition B	% of composition C	% of composition D
cement	45	50	60	
sand	45		30	19
gravel	10	20		1
mass needed to break test bar (kg)	200	50	185	40

Module 4 — Harnessing Chemicals

Rates of Reaction

Q1 Mike works for a **pharmaceutical company**. His job is to **refine** the chemical processes the company uses to increase **profitability**. This often involves maximising the **rate of a reaction**.

a) Which of the following statement(s) correctly define the term 'rate of a chemical reaction'? Tick all that apply.

- The amount of precipitate that is formed. ☐
- The amount of product formed divided by the time taken. ☐
- How fast the reactants are changed into products. ☐
- How quickly the reactants mix together. ☐

b) Mike is currently working on the reaction:

aluminium (s) + hydrochloric acid (aq) → hydrogen (g) + aluminium trichloride (aq)

Complete the diagram below to show how Mike could measure the rate of this reaction.

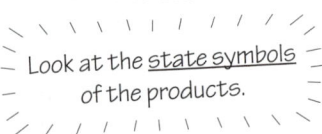

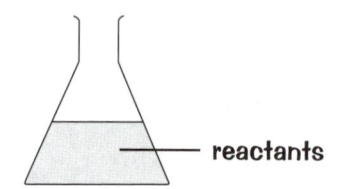

Look at the state symbols of the products.

— reactants

Q2 Ralph is investigating how the **rate of a reaction** depends on the **concentration** of acid he uses. Ralph measures the **volume of gas** produced in **20 seconds** using three different concentrations of acid. His results are shown below.

Reaction	1	2	3
Volume of gas produced (cm³)	80	200	40
Rate (cm³/s)	4		

a) Complete the table with the rates of the second two reactions.

b) In which reaction did Ralph use the **most concentrated acid**? Explain your answer.

Rate = amount of product / time

....

....

c) Ralph repeated reaction 1 using a **catalyst**. What effect would this have on the volume of gas produced in 20 seconds? Circle the correct answer.

        increase it   no change   decrease it

Module 4 — Harnessing Chemicals

Rates of Reaction

Q3 **Silver nitrate** is used in **photographic imaging**. It is made by reacting silver with nitric acid.

silver (s) + nitric acid (aq) → silver nitrate (aq) + nitric oxide (g) + water (l)

The graph below shows how the mass of a reaction batch changed as the reaction progressed.

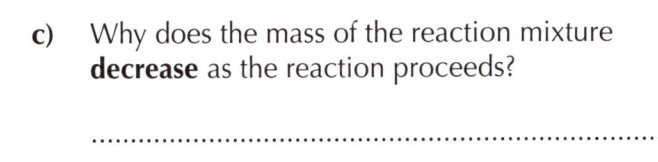

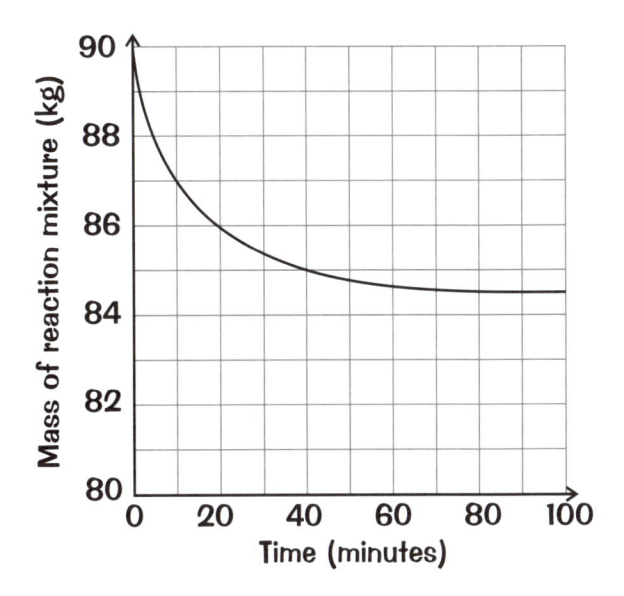

a) What mass of reactants was **lost** in the first **10 minutes** of the reaction?

....

b) How long did it take for the reaction mixture to lose **5 kg**?

....

c) Why does the mass of the reaction mixture **decrease** as the reaction proceeds?

....

....

d) Manufacturers of silver nitrate control the rate of the reaction to make sure it is profitable. Suggest **two** ways to speed up the reaction.

....

....

Q4 Use the words provided to complete the sentences below about measuring rates of reaction.

faster   speed   volume   reactants   gas   mass   formed   precipitation

In a .... reaction you usually measure how quickly the product is formed.

The product turns the solution cloudy. The .... it turns cloudy the quicker

the reaction. In a reaction that produces a .... you can measure how quickly the

.... of the reactants changes or measure the .... of gas given

off in a certain time interval.

Top Tips: If you can't read graphs and tables, you'll struggle with questions about rates of reactions. Never fear though — all it takes is practice and you'll be an expert. Bored, but an expert.

Module 4 — Harnessing Chemicals

Rates of Reaction

Q5 Barium sulfate is used as a white pigment in paints. It can be made inside a fume cupboard using the reaction shown below.

barium chloride(aq) + sulfuric acid(aq) → barium sulfate(s) + hydrochloric acid(aq)

a) Describe a method that could be used to **monitor** the rate of this reaction.

....

....

One of the products is a solid — the reactants are both solutions.

b) Barium sulfate was made using the reaction above, under four different sets of conditions. The curves A to D on the graph below show the rates of the four reactions.

Draw lines to match the conditions described below with the curves on the graph.

- room temperature — A
- high temperature with a catalyst and increased amounts of barium chloride and sulfuric acid — B
- high temperature — C
- high temperature with a catalyst — D

c) What is meant by the term '**catalyst**'?

....

Q6 Coal is used as a fuel in power stations and people's homes. When it burns, a chemical reaction called combustion is taking place.

In a power station, the coal is ground up into a fine powder. In the home, coal is used in lumps. How will the **size** of the pieces of coal used affect the rate of combustion?

....

....

Module 4 — Harnessing Chemicals

Sustainable Chemical Production

Q1 The statements below describe ways to increase the **profitability** of **chemical production**. Tick the boxes of any steps that will also improve the **sustainability** of production.

Changing the supplier of raw materials to a company that offers cheaper products. ☐

Using catalysts instead of high temperatures to increase the rate of reactions. ☐

Carrying out processes during the night when electricity is cheaper. ☐

Switching to alternative reactions that produce fewer waste products. ☐

Selling any useful waste products to other companies rather than disposing of them. ☐

Q2 **Polychloroprene** is a synthetic **rubber**. The raw material used to make it is **crude oil**. Its production requires lots of **energy**.

a) The energy required to make polychloroprene often comes from **burning fossil fuels**. Why is this not a sustainable process?

....

b) Polychloroprene is an alternative to natural rubber, which is collected from rubber trees. Explain why producing **natural** rubber is **more sustainable** than manufacturing polychloroprene.

....

....

Q3 Timothy, a **research chemist**, is investigating three different **methods** of producing hydrochloric acid. His results are shown in the table below.

Method	Theoretical yield (kg)	Actual yield (kg)	Percentage yield
A	56	23.5	
B	84	38	
C	28	17	

a) i) Fill in the table by calculating the percentage yield of each method.

ii) Based on the information in the table, which method would Timothy be most interested in? ....

$\%\ \text{yield} = \dfrac{\text{actual yield}}{\text{theoretical yield}}$

b) Suggest **two** other factors Timothy would consider when choosing a method to use on a **large scale**.

....

....

Module 4 — Harnessing Chemicals

Sustainable Chemical Production

Q4 The diagrams below show the **reactions** used in four common **industrial processes**.

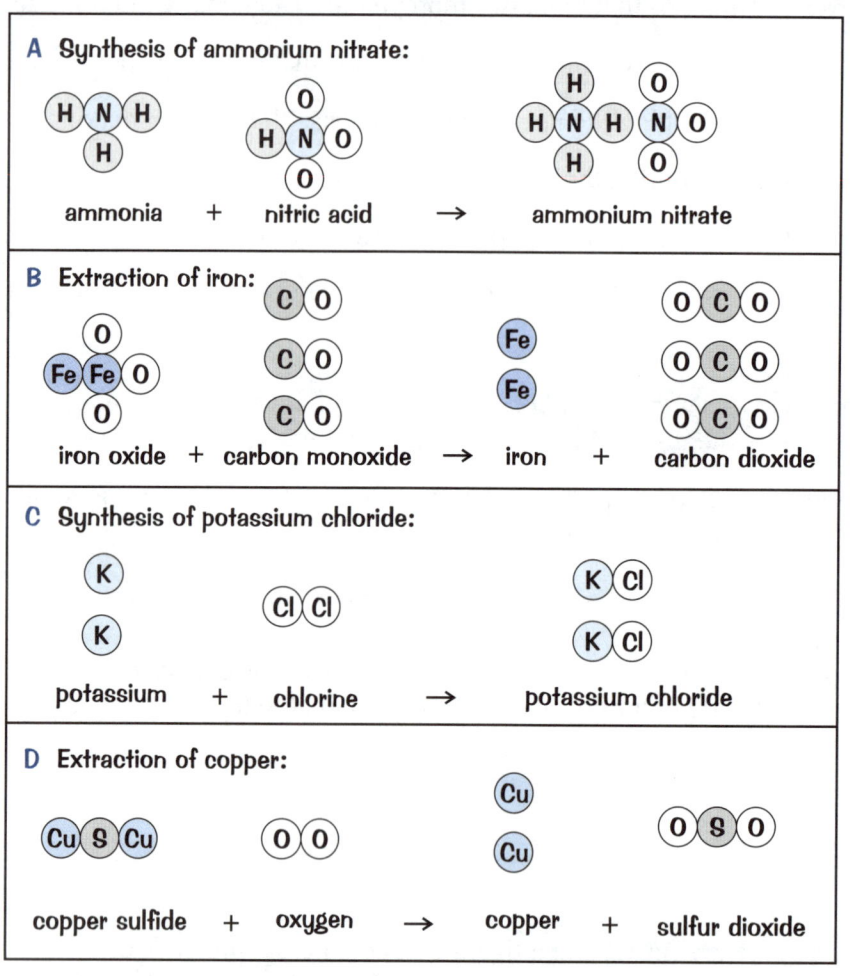

A Synthesis of ammonium nitrate:

ammonia + nitric acid → ammonium nitrate

B Extraction of iron:

iron oxide + carbon monoxide → iron + carbon dioxide

C Synthesis of potassium chloride:

potassium + chlorine → potassium chloride

D Extraction of copper:

copper sulfide + oxygen → copper + sulfur dioxide

a) Which of these reactions have **100%** atom economy? Circle the correct answer(s).

A   B   C   D

b) i) Which of the reactions produces the **most waste**? Circle the correct answer.

A   B   C   D

ii) Suggest a way of reducing the negative effect of the waste produced by this reaction.

....

c) This diagram shows an alternative method of making potassium chloride.

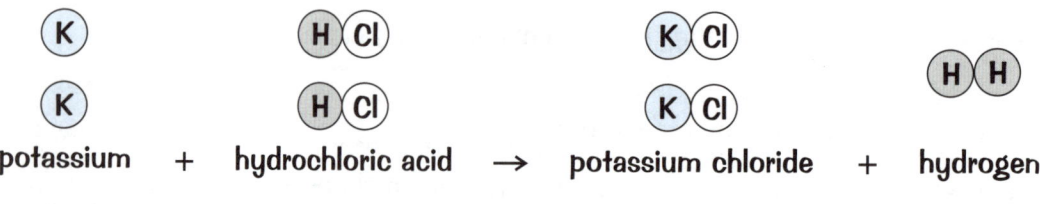

potassium + hydrochloric acid → potassium chloride + hydrogen

Does this have as good an atom economy as process C? Explain your answer.

....

....

Module 4 — Harnessing Chemicals

Chemical Purity

Q1 Magnesium chloride has many uses, for example, it is used to de-ice roads and in the production of soya milk.

The boxes below give information about different **grades** of magnesium chloride, but the information is jumbled up.

analytical grade	High purity	£78 per kg
technical grade	Moderate purity	£3 per kg
laboratory grade	Low purity	£17 per kg

a) Draw lines to match the grade, purity and price of each product.

b) Why would laboratory grade magnesium chloride not be the best choice for use as a de-icer?

....

c) Which grade would be used in the manufacture of soya milk? Explain your answer.

....

Q2 The police have discovered a batch of **counterfeit medicines**. They suspect the drugs have been made using **technical grade** chemicals.

a) How would the counterfeiters benefit from using technical grade chemicals?

....

b) Why is it illegal to make medicines from technical grade chemicals?

....

c) Give **one** reason why medicines are usually expensive to buy.

....

....

d) Name another type of product that would be made using only the purest chemicals.

....

Top Tips: Working out how pure a chemical needs to be for a particular use is mainly common sense, but not always. For example, you'd think tap water that's safe to **drink** would be fine for **rinsing an insoluble salt** you've just made, but no... tap water contains lots of impurities that might **react** with your lovely salt. That's why you'd use much purer, distilled water for that kind of thing.

Module 4 — Harnessing Chemicals

Industrial Production of Chemicals

Q1 Some **bulk chemicals**, some **fine chemicals** and their **uses** are given below.

ammonia — fertiliser

phosphoric acid — fertiliser manufacture

sulfuric acid — detergent manufacture

sodium hydroxide — soap manufacture

acetophenone — perfume ingredient

benzaldehyde — food flavouring

aspirin — painkiller

a) Circle the correct word from the pair to complete the following sentence.

A bulk chemical is a chemical that is manufactured on a **large** / **small** scale.

b) Complete the table to show whether each chemical named above is a bulk chemical or fine chemical:

Bulk chemicals	Fine chemicals

Incredible bulk

c) Suggest why fine chemicals are **more expensive** than bulk chemicals.

....

Q2 The four people below work in the **chemical industry**.

Draw lines to match each person's job title with the correct description of their role.

Quality control manager | Process design and refinement scientist | Environmental scientist | Research and development scientist

Ensures that products are consistently of a high quality.

Monitors the environmental impact of the processes used.

Investigates new products and the methods needed for manufacture.

Ensures that the methods used are safe, efficient and profitable on a large scale.

Module 4 — Harnessing Chemicals

Scaling Up

Q1 Clare works in the **research** department of a chemical company. She has helped to design a new process in the **laboratory**. The next stage is to **scale** the process up for **mass production**.

The diagram below shows the laboratory process.

1) Measure out correct quantities of chemicals A and B. 
2) Pour chemicals A and B into a beaker. 
3) Stir the mixture thoroughly. 
4) Separate the product from the by-product and unreacted chemicals.

a) i) Why would **glass** not be a good choice for the reaction vessel in a large scale process?

....

ii) Suggest a more suitable material for the reaction vessel.

....

b) In the lab, Clare pours the reactants into the reaction vessel from test tubes.
How would the chemicals be transferred to the reaction vessel during large scale production?

....

c) Clare uses a stirring rod to mix the chemicals in the lab.
How could the chemicals be mixed during mass production?

....

d) The reaction gives out heat. Describe how the temperature of the reaction vessel could be controlled so that it remains safe.

....

Clare's method uses **two liquid reactants** and produces two products — a **liquid product** and a **solid by-product**.

e) Circle the correct word from each pair to complete the following sentences.

i) The solid by-product can be removed by **filtration** / **distillation**.

ii) Any unreacted reagents left in the reaction mixture can be removed by **filtration** / **distillation**.

Top Tips: The chemical industry doesn't do things by halves. For example, the Contact Process is used to make about 160 million tonnes of sulfuric acid every year. Now that's a whole lot of acid — so unless you want to **waste** a whole lot of **money** it's a good idea to be efficient about it.

Module 4 — Harnessing Chemicals

Planning Chemical Synthesis

Q1 Ethene is used to make the world's biggest selling plastic — polyethene. The diagram below shows two industrial reaction schemes to make ethene.

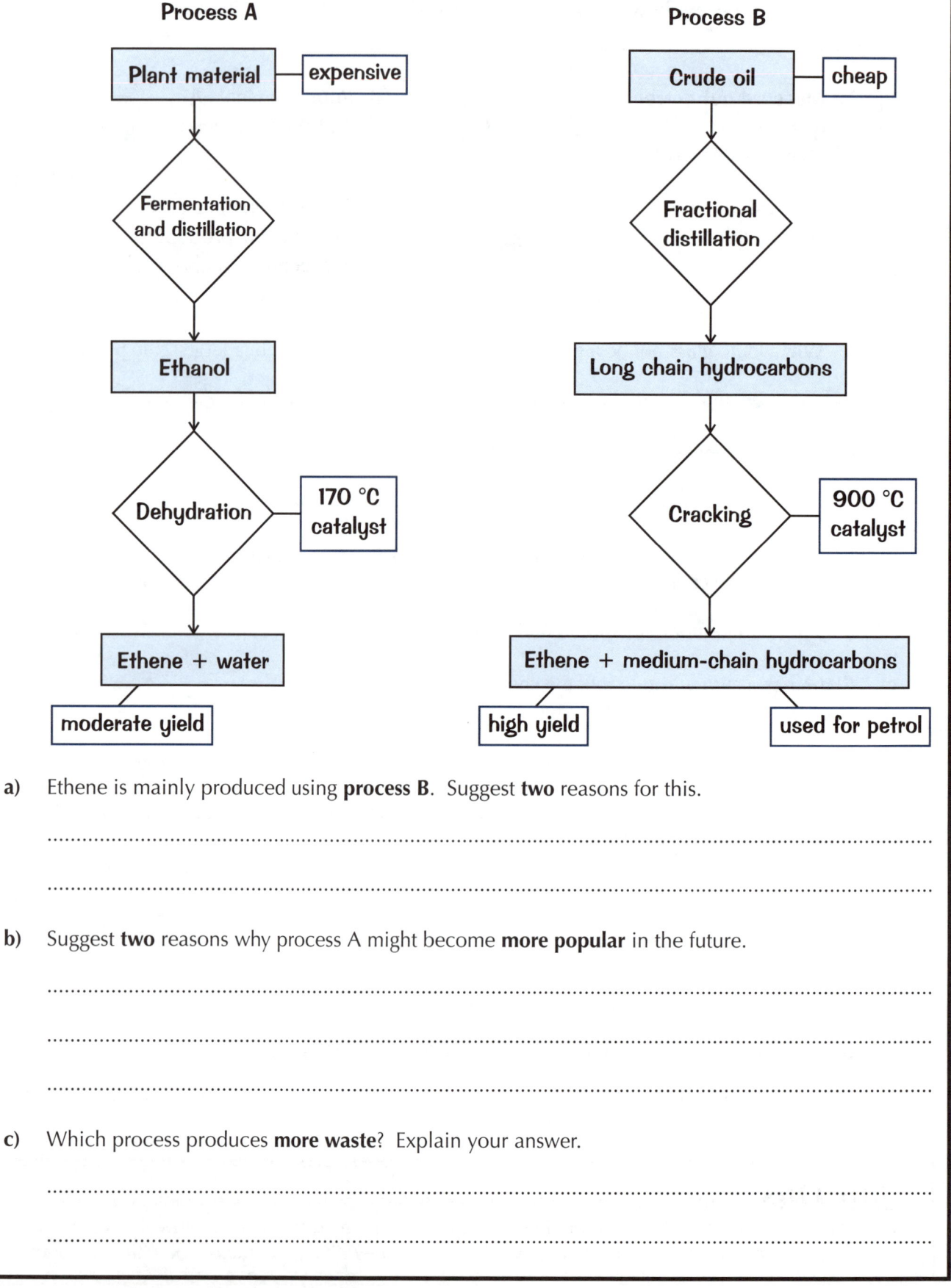

Process A
- Plant material — expensive
- ↓
- Fermentation and distillation
- ↓
- Ethanol
- ↓
- Dehydration — 170 °C catalyst
- ↓
- Ethene + water
- moderate yield

Process B
- Crude oil — cheap
- ↓
- Fractional distillation
- ↓
- Long chain hydrocarbons
- ↓
- Cracking — 900 °C catalyst
- ↓
- Ethene + medium-chain hydrocarbons
- high yield | used for petrol

a) Ethene is mainly produced using **process B**. Suggest **two** reasons for this.

....

....

b) Suggest **two** reasons why process A might become **more popular** in the future.

....

....

....

c) Which process produces **more waste**? Explain your answer.

....

....

Module 4 — Harnessing Chemicals

Planning Chemical Synthesis

Q2 Calcium hydroxide is used in whitewash and plaster as well as in the petroleum industry. It is made by reacting calcium oxide with water.

a) The reaction between calcium oxide and water is **exothermic**. Explain what this means.

....

b) The output of an exothermic reaction can be used to improve the energy efficiency of a chemical plant.

i) Why is it important for a chemical process to be energy efficient? Circle the correct answer(s).

- because using a lot of energy is expensive
- because energy often comes from fossil fuels which damage the environment
- because energy is a non-renewable resource, so will run out
- because it reduces the need for catalysts

ii) Describe how an exothermic reaction can be used to improve energy efficiency.

....

....

c) What is meant by an '**endothermic**' reaction?

....

Q3 Brian works in the process department at a petrochemical factory. He has prepared the information below to help new recruits learn about the work done by his team.

Circle the correct word from each pair to complete the passage.

> There are often many processes we could use to make one of our products. Our job is to make sure the processes we use are **expensive** / **profitable** and **sustainable** / **renewable**. To do this, we try to select processes that use cheap, **renewable** / **non-renewable** raw materials. They should also produce a **high** / **low** yield of the product without needing a large amount of energy. We also try to choose processes with **high** / **low** atom economy, as this minimises the cost and environmental issues of dealing with waste products.

Top Tips:
There are four main things to think about when a company chooses a particular manufacturing process — yield, costs, energy requirements and what to do with any waste. Learn why each is important, then have a think about how to synthesise a cup of tea and a biscuit.

Module 4 — Harnessing Chemicals

Testing Formulations

Q1 The table below shows the results of a **quality control** test at **Pete's Paints**.

	Ideal paint	Batch A	Batch B	Batch C
Binder	40	30	41	45
Pigment	10	10	9	5
Solvent	50	60	50	50

a) Which of the batches is closest to the ideal composition? ....

b) The binder is used to hold the coloured pigment particles together. The amount of solvent controls the thickness of the paint — the more solvent there is, the thinner the paint.

　i) Which batch of paint will probably be too runny? ....

　ii) Which batch of paint will not be the right colour? ....

c) Give **two** reasons why companies test their products before they go on sale.

....

....

Q2 Ails Away is developing a new **flu remedy**. They test three formulations on groups of **volunteers**. Each person fills in a **questionnaire** rating how well the remedy eased their **symptoms**.

The table below shows the average scores for each remedy tested. Scores go from 0 to 5, with 0 being no change and 5 meaning the symptoms disappeared completely.

Symptom	Remedy A	Remedy B	Remedy C
Blocked nose	2	3	4
Sinus pain	1	4	3
Headaches	1	4	4

a) Which formulation(s) should the company continue to develop?　　A　　B　　C

b) What else would the formulations need to be tested for before they went on sale?

....

c) Before the remedy went on sale it would be tested to ensure it met the national standards. Why is it important to have national standards for products like this?

....

....

Module 4 — Harnessing Chemicals

Regulating the Chemical Industry

Q1 Complete the passage below by circling the correct word from each pair.

> The Government sets strict laws about the **processing** / prices, storage and naming / **transport** of chemicals. The aim is to keep workers and the public safe by increasing / **limiting** people's exposure to dangerous chemicals. The laws also protect the **environment** / economy by controlling the transport of hazardous chemicals. There are also guidelines for handling chemicals safely. Their purpose is to increase / **decrease** the chance of accidents happening and minimise the cost / **damage** caused if an accident does happen.

Q2 Tick the boxes to show whether the following statements about the **Health and Safety Executive** (HSE) are **true** or **false**.

		True	False
a)	The HSE is only concerned with keeping workers safe.	☐	☐
b)	The HSE checks that chemical companies follow the safety rules.	☐	☐
c)	The HSE makes sure that workers don't have to use dangerous chemicals.	☐	☐
d)	The HSE aims to minimise the risks of chemicals to workers and the public.	☐	☐

Q3 Dave is a **HSE inspector**. He has identified some problems at a chemical plant. Draw lines to match each problem described below with the appropriate **action** Dave should take.

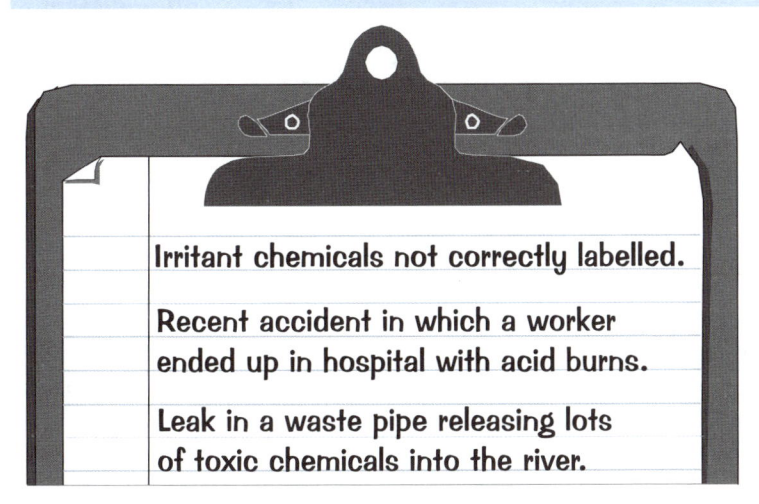

Problems:
- Irritant chemicals not correctly labelled.
- Recent accident in which a worker ended up in hospital with acid burns.
- Leak in a waste pipe releasing lots of toxic chemicals into the river.

Actions:
- Shut down the plant. Reopen only when the fault has been dealt with satisfactorily.
- Investigate circumstances then give appropriate advice to prevent problem happening again.
- Advise the company on how to put the fault right.

Top Tips: Rules and regulations aren't the most exciting topics in the world, but they are useful. The important things to remember is who makes the rules — the Government — and why they make them — so that we're all safe from the dangerous effects of some chemicals.

Module 4 — Harnessing Chemicals

Mixed Questions for Module 4

Q1 Nitric acid is used in the manufacture of fertilisers and explosives.

a) Nitric acid will corrode living tissue. Circle the correct hazard symbol for nitric acid.

b) What reading would nitric acid give on a pH meter? Circle the correct answer.

   1-2   **6.5-7.5**   **12-13**

c) The equipment shown below is used to react sodium hydroxide with nitric acid.

   i) Name the pieces of equipment labelled on the diagram.

   A ....

   B ....

   C ....

   ii) What type of reaction is taking place?

   ....

   iii) What will be the pH of the solution when the reaction is complete?

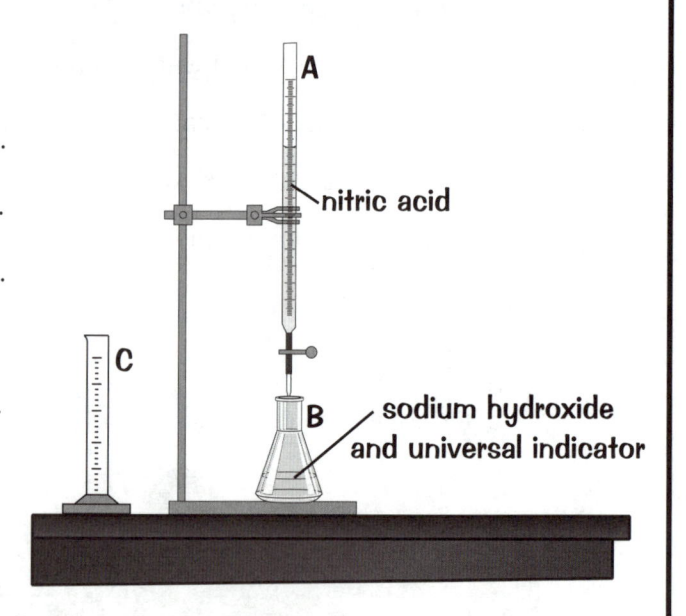

   ....

   iv) Describe how the reaction could be monitored to show when it is complete.

   ....

   v) What are the products of the reaction?

   ....

d) Complete the following word equations.

   i) nitric acid + calcium → ....

   ii) nitric acid + magnesium carbonate → ....

Module 4 — Harnessing Chemicals

Mixed Questions for Module 4

Q2 **Copper chloride** can be prepared by mixing copper oxide and hydrochloric acid, as shown in steps A and B below, then following the further steps C and D.

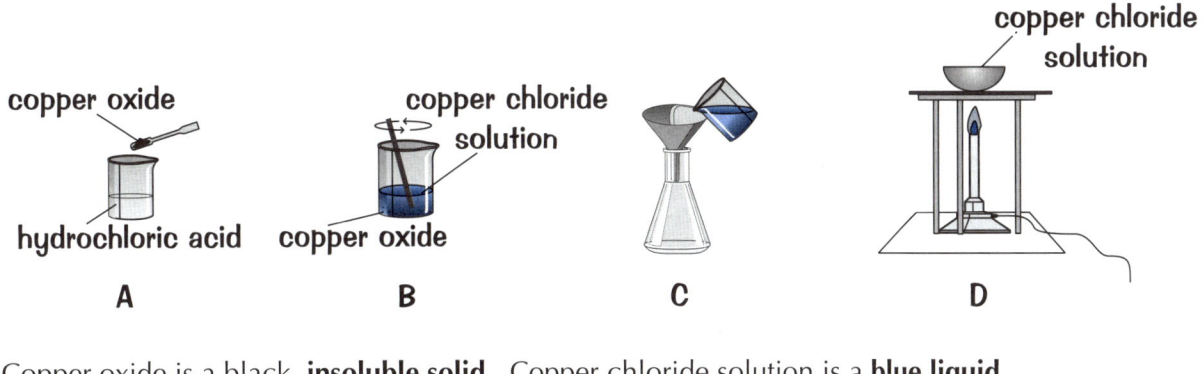

A: copper oxide, hydrochloric acid
B: copper chloride solution, copper oxide
C: (filtration apparatus)
D: copper chloride solution (evaporation)

Copper oxide is a black, **insoluble solid**. Copper chloride solution is a **blue liquid**.

a) How can you be sure that all the hydrochloric acid has reacted?

....

b) Name process C and explain why it is necessary. ....

....

c) i) Describe how crystals of copper chloride are obtained in process D.

....

ii) How could **larger** crystals of copper chloride be obtained?

....

The graph below shows the concentration of copper chloride solution as the reaction progresses.

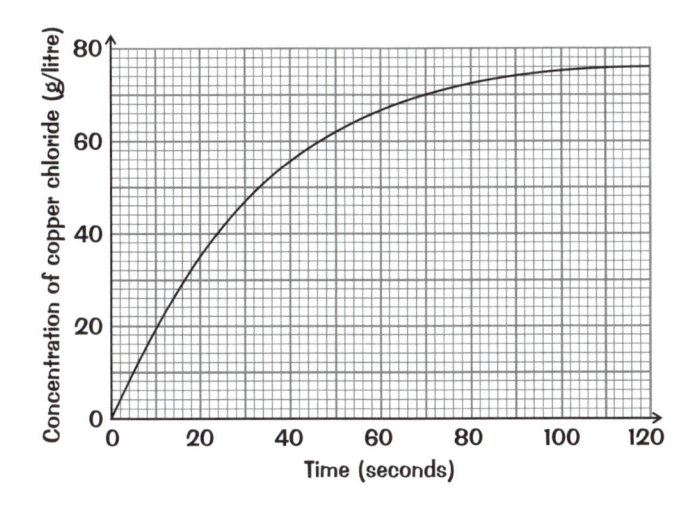

d) What is the concentration of copper chloride solution after 50 seconds?

....

e) How long does it take for the concentration to reach 40 g/litre?

....

f) What is the final concentration of copper chloride solution?

....

g) Give **two** ways in which the rate of the reaction could be increased.

....

....

Module 4 — Harnessing Chemicals

Mixed Questions for Module 4

Q3 Hazleen is devoping a form of the painkiller **ibuprofen** that can be given to **children**.

a) The raw material used to make ibuprofen is crude oil. What does this show about ibuprofen? Circle the correct answer.

   it is an organic chemical   **it is an inorganic chemical**

b) There are two different processes, A and B, that Hazleen could use to manufacture ibuprofen. The atom economy of process A is 40% and the atom economy of process B is 77%.

   i) Based on the **atom economy**, which process is more sustainable? Explain your answer.

   ....

   ....

   ii) Give **three** things, other than atom economy, that Hazleen should consider when choosing which process to use.

   ....

   ....

c) The chemical formula for ibuprofen is $C_{13}H_{18}O_2$.
   List the names and number of atoms of the elements in a molecule of ibuprofen.

   ....

d) Ibuprofen is a '**fine**' chemical. Explain what this means.

   ....

e) Hazleen's final product consists of solid particles of ibuprofen dispersed in a syrupy liquid. What type of mixture is this? Circle the correct answer.

   extrusion   suspension   emulsion   solution

f) What **grade** of chemicals should Hazleen use to manufacture the product? Give a reason for your answer.

   ....

   ....

g) The concentration of ibuprofen in the product is 20 g/litre.
   Calculate the mass of ibuprofen contained in a 2.5 ml dose.

   ....

h) The product will undergo a series of tests before it is allowed to go on sale.
   Give **two** reasons why it will be tested.

   ....

   ....

Module 4 — Harnessing Chemicals

Module 5 — Communications

Communicating Information

Q1 There are many different ways of **communicating information**. Some examples are given below.

digital television   telephone   smoke detector   hazard warning sign

a) Name one example above that uses **sound** to convey information.

....

b) Which example above receives information in the form of a **code**?

....

c) i) The hazard warning sign uses a **visual symbol**. Give another example of communication device not pictured above that uses a visual symbol.

....

ii) Describe one advantage of using visual symbols to convey information.

....

....

Q2 **Semaphore** is a system of communication that uses the position of **flags** to represent letters of the alphabet. The use of semaphore was once common, but it has now been replaced by **modern** technologies such as **telephones**. It is still used by emergency personnel in some situations.

CGP... well what else would we write...

a) Give two advantages of using a telephone instead of semaphore.

1. ....

2. ....

b) Why can semaphore still be useful in some situations?

....

....

Top Tips: Learning advantages and disadvantages of communications devices might be less appealing than broccoli ice-cream, but the examiners seem to think it's something you should know.

Module 5 — Communications

110

The Communications Industry

Q1 **Electronic technologies** can be used to **improve communications** between people.

a) Do the technologies below increase the **quality**, **quantity** or **distance** of communication? Draw lines to match each technology to the best answer.

mobile phone	increases distance of communication
hearing aid	increases quantity of communication
international television broadcast	increases quality of communication

b) Suggest another technology that has increased the **quantity** of communication between people.

....

c) Give one way that using a hearing aid might make life easier for someone with hearing difficulties.

....

d) Describe one benefit of international television broadcasts.

....

Q2 The government encourages **competition** between telecommunications firms, such as mobile phone companies or internet service providers.

Explain why competition between companies is good for customers.

....

....

Q3 **Air traffic controllers** send information to pilots about their route and the weather conditions. These messages must be transmitted using a **standard DIS protocol**.

a) Using a standard protocol ensures that data is communicated reliably. What is a standard protocol? Circle the correct letter from the list below.

    A   A set of rules for how air traffic controllers should behave.

    B   A set of rules for how data is sent over a communications system.

    C   A set of instructions for using a communications system.

    D   A way of encrypting data.

b) Explain why it is important that other communications systems, such as mobile phones and radio broadcasts, do **not** use the same frequency as air traffic controllers.

....

....

Module 5 — Communications

Designing Communication Systems

Q1 A **mobile phone manufacturer** is designing an environmentally friendly mobile phone that will use **solar power** and be made of **recycled materials**. The company is deciding on the **product specification**.

a) What is a product specification? Circle the correct letter from the list below.

   A   A description of how a product will be made.

   B   A description of how a product is special.

   C   A description of the costs involved in making and using a product.

   D   A description of the key features of a product.

b) Suggest **three** factors that should be described in the new phone's product specification.

   1. ....

   2. ....

   3. ....

c) The solar cells needed cost several hundred pounds. The manager decides that if this cost cannot be reduced, the phone will not be made. Explain why the manager has made this decision.

   ....

   ....

Q2 Communications products are designed to meet the needs of the **customer**. The words in the list below are **features** that certain customers will find appealing.

   durable   fashionable   reliable   multi-function   colour screen   weather resistant

A market researcher interviewed a sample of people about what features they want their communications products to have. Below are two responses. For each, suggest three features from the list above that you would include in a product designed to appeal to this person.

a) "I like to listen to music and play games on my mobile. It's got to look modern and stylish too."

....

b) "When we're out on the hills, it's really useful to have two-way radios to keep in touch with each other in case of an emergency."

....

Module 5 — Communications

Designing Communication Systems

Q3 The **fire alarms** at a **school** need to be replaced. The table below compares the features of two fire alarms that the school could choose.

Feature	Fire Alarm SS45	Fire Alarm MX43
Mass	300 g	400 g
Dimensions	80 × 130 × 50 mm	90 × 150 × 60 mm
Alarm type	85 decibel local alarm. Sends message to emergency services.	90 decibel local alarm. Sends message to emergency services.
Power supply	Mains-powered, battery back-up	Battery-powered
Additional features	Low-battery warning, tamper-resistant	Low-battery warning, remote control testing
Cost per unit	£40	£35

a) Suggest why the fire alarms used in schools send a message to the emergency services as well as making a loud noise.

....

....

b) One of the fire alarms is battery-powered and the other is powered by the mains.

　i) Explain the advantage of powering fire alarms from the mains supply.

....

　ii) Explain why it is important that mains-powered fire alarms have a battery back-up.

....

c) i) Give **one** reason why Fire Alarm SS45 might be chosen by the school.

....

　ii) Give **one** reason why Fire Alarm MX23 might be chosen by the school.

....

Top Tips: There are loads of things that manufacturers need to weigh up before the final specification of a product is decided on. Because the specifications tell you about the key features, they can be really useful when you're in a right muddle trying to decide which product to buy.

Module 5 — Communications

Jobs in the Communications Industry

Q1 CGP Broadcasting is a company that provides **outside broadcasting facilities** to television and radio stations. They rent out fully-equipped broadcasting vans, with or without experienced broadcasting crews. A picture of one of their outside broadcasting vans is shown below.

a) What is the function of:

i) the van's transmitter,

....

ii) a domestic TV receiver.

....

b) The van contains a workspace for all the members of a broadcasting crew. The sound engineer works in the audio section of the van.

i) Describe the role of the sound engineer.

....

ii) Give **two** examples of pieces of equipment the sound engineer might use.

1. ....

2. ....

iii) Suggest **two** skills needed by a sound engineer.

1. ....

2. ....

c) Suggest the job titles of two other members of a broadcasting crew and describe each of their jobs.

Job title 1: ....

Description: ....

Job title 2: ....

Description: ....

Module 5 — Communications

Health and Safety

Q1 Ellen works for a company that manufactures **computer equipment**. Her workplace contains **safety symbols**, and some of the equipment produced also has to be marked with safety symbols.

   a) Match up the following safety symbols found in Ellen's workplace with their correct definition.

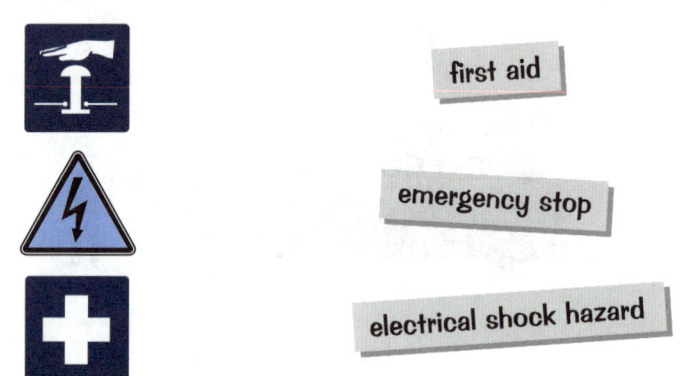

   - first aid
   - emergency stop
   - electrical shock hazard

   b) The CD drives produced by Ellen's company are marked with the following safety symbol:

   i) What **hazard** do the CD drives contain?

   ....

   ii) What is the **risk** associated with this hazard?

   ....

Q2 Martin is a **telecommunications engineer**. He is repairing an overhead phone line.

   a) Martin has to put a hazard warning sign on the ground underneath where he is working. The sign uses the general danger symbol, and writing underneath it explains that he is working overhead.

   i) Complete the diagram by drawing the general danger symbol on the sign.

   Man working overhead

   ii) What is the risk to people on the ground when Martin is working overhead?

   ....

   b) When Martin works on overhead phone lines, there is a risk he will fall and injure himself. Suggest one way Martin can reduce this risk.

   ....

Module 5 — Communications

Health and Safety

Q3 Samantha is installing a **burglar alarm**. She notices it has the following two symbols on it.

A ♥ B ▣

a) What does symbol A tell Samantha about the alarm?
Circle the correct letter from the list below:

- **A** The alarm is safe to use.
- **B** The alarm has met European safety standards.
- **C** The alarm is safe to install.
- **D** The alarm has met British safety standards.

b) Symbol B tells Samantha that the alarm has a built-in safety feature.

  i) What safety feature does symbol B indicate? ....

  ii) Explain how this safety feature works.

  ....

  ....

c) Suggest one other built-in safety feature the alarm might have. ....

Q4 The **Health and Safety Executive** has published a leaflet describing five steps to **risk assessment**.

> 1. Identify hazards.
> 2. Decide who might be harmed and how.
> 3. Assess the risk and decide on precautions.
> 4. Record findings and implement them.
> 5. Review assessment regularly.

a) Step 3 involves assessing a risk. What are the two most important things you should consider when assessing a risk?

1. ....

2. ....

b) Assess the risk involved in the following activities. Circle whether you think they are low risk, medium risk or high risk.

  i) Watching a digital television.   low risk / medium risk / high risk

  ii) Using hand-held tools to repair a telephone.   low risk / medium risk / high risk

  iii) Installing a satellite dish on a roof.   low risk / medium risk / high risk

Module 5 — Communications

Flowcharts and Datasheets

Q1 The **flowchart** below can be used to help customers find the **most suitable communications device** to use at work.

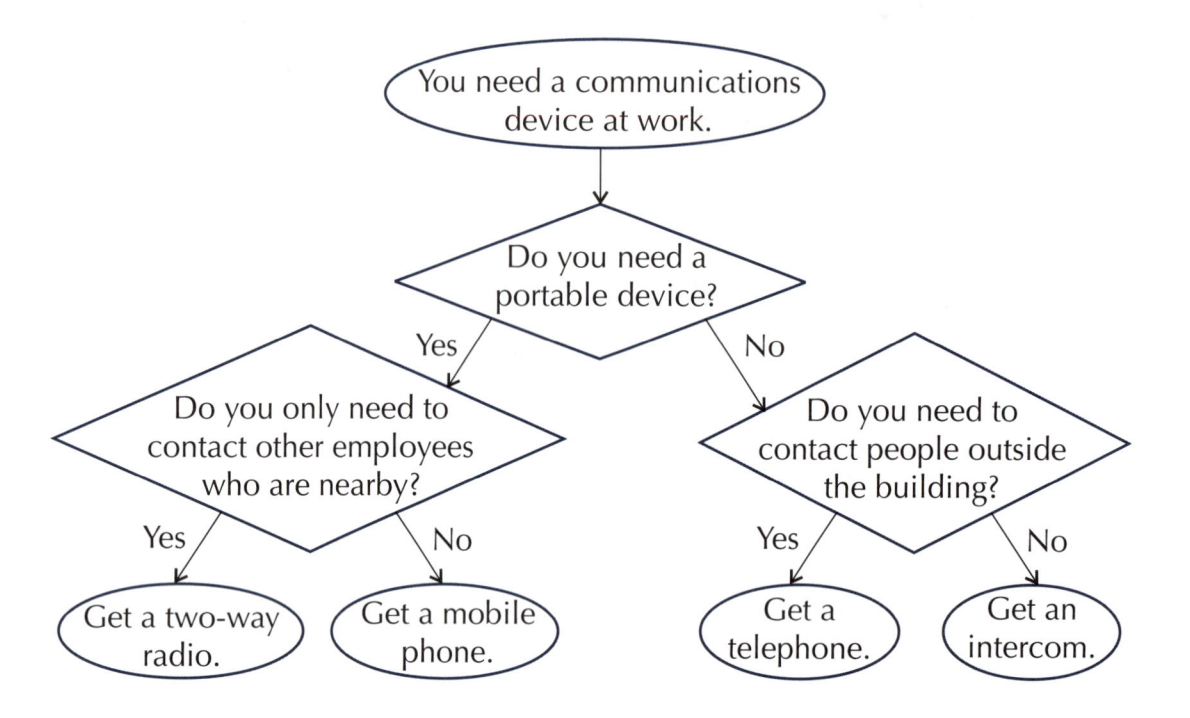

```
You need a communications device at work.
                |
                v
        Do you need a portable device?
       Yes /              \ No
          v                v
  Do you only need to     Do you need to
  contact other employees  contact people outside
  who are nearby?          the building?
   Yes /    \ No          Yes /    \ No
      v      v               v      v
  Get a    Get a mobile    Get a    Get an
  two-way  phone.          telephone. intercom.
  radio.
```

a) Describe how **oval** shapes and **diamond** shapes are used in the flowchart.

....

....

b) Security guards need to carry a communications device with them that allows them to contact other security guards nearby. Use the flowchart to find the most suitable communications device.

....

c) Most of the workers in a bank only need to contact other workers in the same building. However, the managers need to be able to contact customers. Suggest a communications device that would be suitable for:

i) the majority of the workers,

....

ii) the managers.

....

Top Tips: Flowcharts are pretty useful things — they can help you find answers to questions. You only need to start getting worried when you notice that you're running your whole life using flowcharts. "Should I have bacon for breakfast?" "Should I change my name to Jean Poole?"

Module 5 — Communications

Flowcharts and Datasheets

Q2 A company that manufactures miniature electronic amplifiers has created a **datasheet** to give customers information about their products.

A customer compares the information about three models of amplifier shown in the datasheet below.

	Amplifier 1	Amplifier 2	Amplifier 3
Supply voltage (V)	2.5 - 4	2.5 - 4	2.5 - 5.5
Power output (mW)	500	750	1000
Maximum distortion (%)	1	1.5	2
Cost (£)	2	3	4

A higher power output means a greater maximum volume.

a) The customer wants an amplifier with a power output of at least **700 mW**. He doesn't want to spend more than **£3**. Which amplifier would be the best choice?

....

b) Describe one advantage of Amplifier 1 compared to the other two models.

....

c) Describe one advantage and one disadvantage of Amplifier 3 compared to the other two models.

....

....

Q3 Omar needs to buy a new **battery** for his **mobile phone**.

He is considering the following models.

	Battery 1	Battery 2	Battery 3
Recharged by	Wind-up mechanism	Mains supply	Mains supply
Talk time	30 minutes	2 hours	4 hours
Cost	£50	£10	£20

a) Describe one difference between Battery 2 and Battery 3.

....

b) Omar decides to buy both Battery 1 and Battery 3. Suggest why he bought both models.

....

....

Module 5 — Communications

Block Diagrams

Q1 **Block diagrams** are one way of **representing systems**. They simplify systems by breaking them down into a series of simple units called **blocks**.

   a) What do the **blocks** represent? Choose the correct answer from the list below:

   A   processes

   B   data

   C   microchips

   D   products

   b) What do the **arrows** between blocks show? Choose the correct answer from the list below:

   A   the flow of current

   B   the flow of voltage

   C   the flow of information

   D   the direction of waves

   c) Complete the block diagram below by labelling the **input** device, the **output** device and the **processor**.

   [ ] → [ ] → [ ]

Q2 Richard has drawn a block diagram of his **radio**.

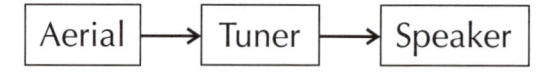

   Aerial → Tuner → Speaker

   a) What is the input device? ....

   b) Explain what the input device does by completing the sentence using words from below.

   electrical signals   electrical waves   sound signals   radio waves

   The input device converts .... into ....

   c) Explain what the output device does.

   ....

   d) What transports information from the aerial to the tuner, and from the tuner to the speaker?

   ....

Module 5 — Communications

Block Diagrams

Q3 Fax machines contain a **scanner**, **modem** and **printer**, and can send images along telephone lines.

Draw a block diagram that shows how information is sent from one fax machine to another.

Q4 Thomas wears a **hearing aid** to increase the volume of sounds.

a) Draw lines to match each function to the correct hearing aid component.

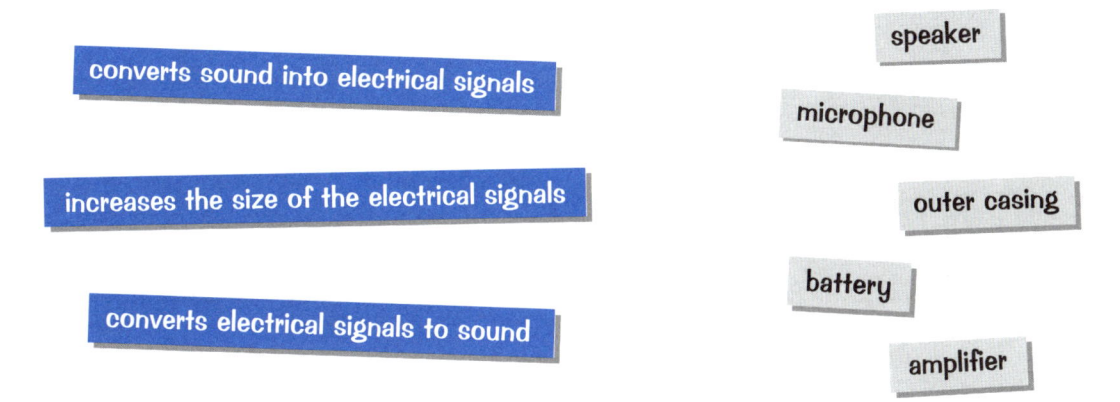

converts sound into electrical signals

increases the size of the electrical signals

converts electrical signals to sound

speaker
microphone
outer casing
battery
amplifier

b) Label the block diagram of a hearing aid below with the correct components.

☐ → ☐ → ☐

c) Thomas's hearing aid has broken, so he takes it to Glyn for repair. Glyn tests each of the components of the broken hearing aid one by one. The table below shows the results of his investigation.

Component	Working?
Speaker	No
Microphone	Yes
Amplifier	Yes

Glyn decides to replace a wire between two of the components. Describe the location of the wire he should replace.

....

Top Tips: Block diagrams simply break complex electronic systems into simple units — sometimes as few as three. And just in case you haven't had quite enough fun with block diagrams yet, turn over and there's a fantastic surprise waiting for you... What more could you want...

Module 5 — Communications

Block Diagrams

Q5 A hospital has a **fire alarm system** that alerts the fire brigade when it is triggered.

a) Complete the block diagram for the system by using words from the box below. You can use any of the words more than once.

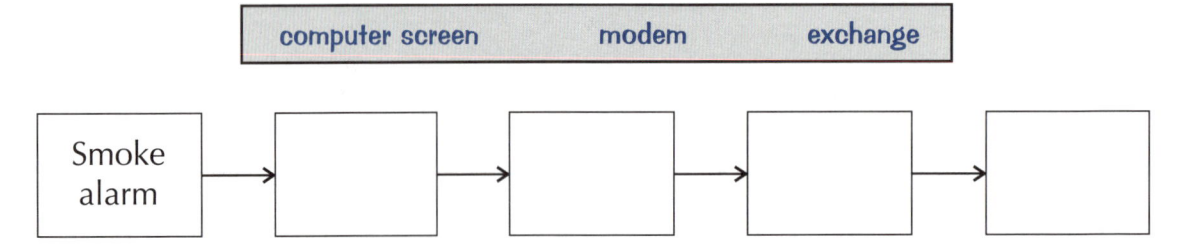

> computer screen   modem   exchange

Smoke alarm → ☐ → ☐ → ☐ → ☐

b) Identify the:

   i) input device ....

   ii) processors ....

   iii) output device ....

c) Explain what the input device does.

   ....

Q6 An **e-mail communications system** can be represented by the block diagram below.

Keyboard → CPU → Modem → Exchange → Modem → CPU → Monitor

a) What is the input device? Circle the correct letter from the list below.

   A   a computer monitor   B   a person
   C   a keyboard   D   a CPU

b) Describe the role of the CPU.

   ....

c) Name the output device.

   ....

d) Jackie sends an e-mail to a friend. She receives confirmation from the exchange that the message was sent. However, her friend does not receive the message. Suggest which part of the communications system might be faulty.

   ....

Module 5 — Communications

Circuit Diagrams

Q1 Lee has made a simple **radio**. A **block diagram** and a **circuit diagram** are shown below.

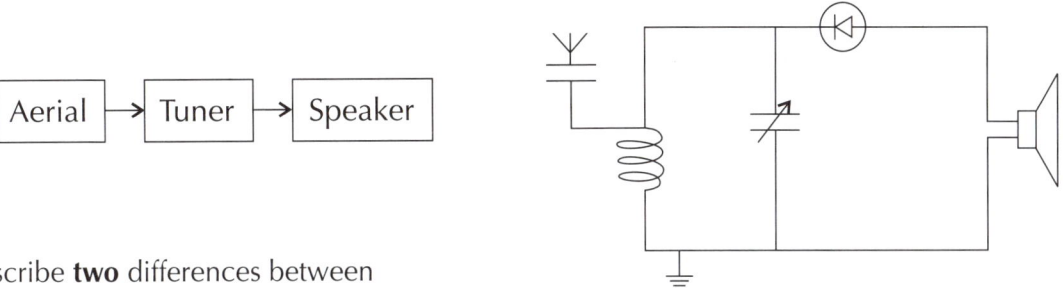

a) Describe **two** differences between circuit diagrams and block diagrams.

1. ....

2. ....

b) Lee wants to measure the current in the circuit and the voltage across the speaker.

i) What should Lee use to measure current? ....

ii) What should Lee use to measure voltage? ....

iii) He can use this information to find the speaker's resistance. Draw lines to match up current, voltage and resistance to their correct definitions and units of measurement.

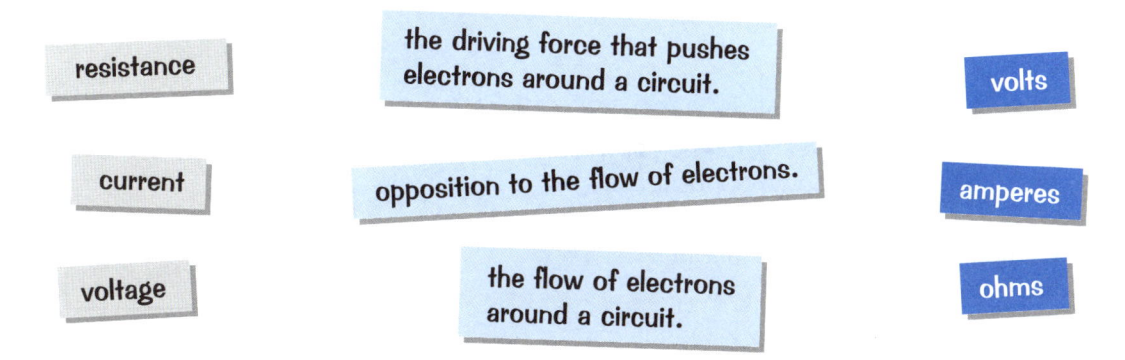

- resistance
- current
- voltage

- the driving force that pushes electrons around a circuit.
- opposition to the flow of electrons.
- the flow of electrons around a circuit.

- volts
- amperes
- ohms

Q2 Mohammad is given the components below to make a circuit with a **buzzer**.

Use the symbols to draw a circuit diagram for a buzzer.

Make sure you put the ammeter and the voltmeter in appropriate places.

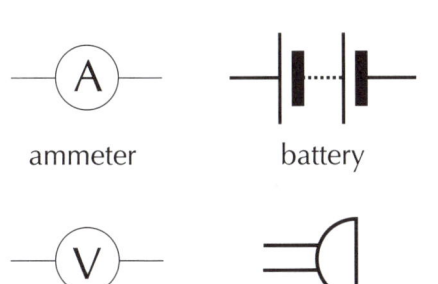

- ammeter
- battery
- voltmeter
- buzzer

Module 5 — Communications

Circuit Diagrams

Q3 Tasha learns in her science lesson that several types of **resistor** are available.

a) Match up the resistors below with the correct symbols. The first one has been done for you.

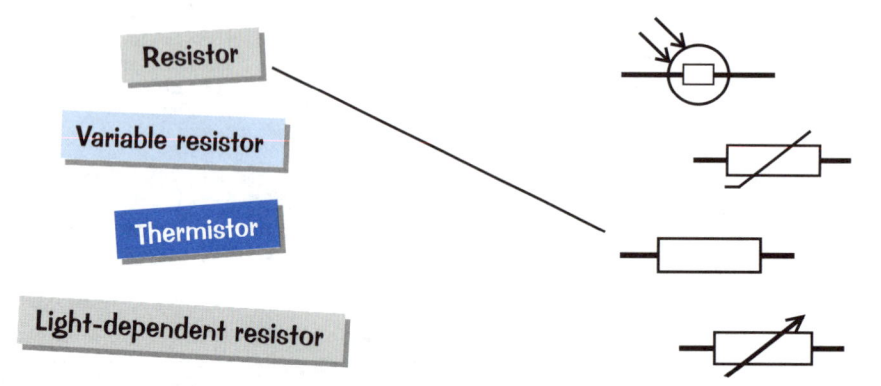

- Resistor
- Variable resistor
- Thermistor
- Light-dependent resistor

b) You can use a variable resistor to control the current in a circuit. What happens to the current if you increase the resistance?

....

c) Which resistor above is likely to be used in a temperature sensor? ....

d) Suggest one use of a light-dependent resistor.

....

Q4 Froggart's Toy Company have designed a new **radio-controlled car**. The car's **circuit diagram** is shown opposite.

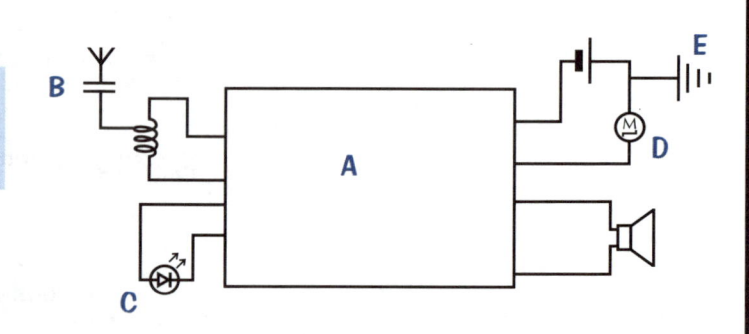

a) Complete the table below about the components of the circuit.

Component	Name	Function
A		A chip that processes information
B	Capacitor	
C	LED	
D		Converts electrical energy to movement
E		

b) Component C is a type of **diode**. Draw the symbol for a **different** type of diode and describe its properties.

Symbol: Properties: ....

....

Module 5 — Communications

Series and Parallel Circuits

Q1 Phil is designing a circuit for a set of **security night lights**. His design is shown below.

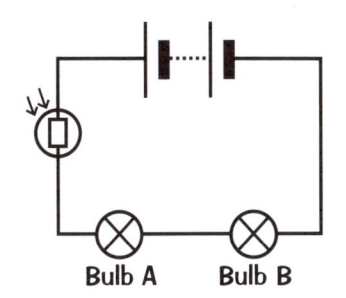

a) Has Phil drawn a series circuit or a parallel circuit?

....

b) The current through the light-dependent resistor is **6 A**. What will the current through Bulb A be? Circle the correct answer.

3 A   6 A   less than 6 A   more than 6 A

c) The battery in the circuit has a voltage of 1.5 V. The voltage across the light-dependent resistor is 0.5 V and the voltage across Bulb A is 0.5 V. What is the voltage across Bulb **B**?

....

d) i) Complete the circuit diagram to show how the same components can be connected in a parallel circuit.

ii) Describe one advantage of connecting all the components in parallel.

....

....

Q2 Ahmet **designs circuits** for his company's products.

a) His first job is to draw a **series circuit** for a cooling fan. Draw a series circuit for the cooling fan using a battery, a switch, a thermistor and a motor.

This isn't a laughing matter...

b) Next, he designs a **parallel circuit** for a lighting system in which three bulbs can be used separately. Draw a parallel circuit using a battery, bulbs and switches for the lighting system.

c) Explain what would happen to the voltage across each component if you added another:

i) motor to the series circuit ....

ii) bulb to the parallel circuit ....

Module 5 — Communications

Series and Parallel Circuits

Q3 Janine sets up a circuit with three **buzzers** connected in **parallel**.

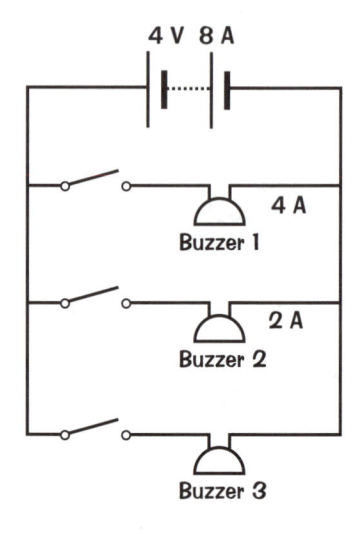

a) What is the advantage of having three switches in a parallel circuit like this?

....

....

b) Use the voltage and current values in the diagram to complete the table below.

	parallel circuit	
	voltage	current
buzzer 1		4 A
buzzer 2		2 A
buzzer 3		

c) Calculate the resistance of buzzer **2**.

....

d) Janine then sets up a series circuit containing the three buzzers.

i) Why does this circuit only need one switch?

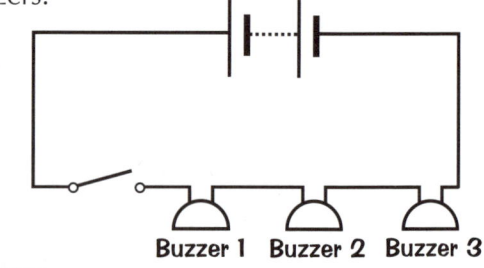

....

....

ii) Janine measures the voltage and current across each buzzer and compares her results with those from her parallel circuit in part b).

	series circuit	
	voltage	current
buzzer 1	0.8 V	0.8 A
buzzer 2	1.6 V	0.8 A
buzzer 3	1.6 V	0.8 A

What conclusions can Janine draw about voltage and current in series and parallel circuits? Complete the passage by circling the correct word(s) in each pair.

> In a parallel circuit, voltage is **the same** / **different** across each component, whereas in series circuits, it is **the same** / **different** across each component. The current through each component in a **series** / **parallel** circuit is different. The current through each component in a **series** / **parallel** circuit is the same.

Module 5 — Communications

Electric Current and Power

Q1 Jim notices that a label on the back of his computer gives information about **power** and **current**.

a) Complete the equations below using words from the box. Words can be used more than once.

| voltage | current | resistance |

i) Current = ... ÷ ....

ii) Power = ... × ....

b) What is **power**? Circle the correct letter from the list below.

A   A measure of the strength of a component.

B   A measure of how quickly energy is transferred.

C   A measure of the force of electricity.

D   A measure of the efficiency of a component.

c) What are the units of power? ....

Q2 The **circuit diagram** for Paul's **audio system** is shown below. The ammeter reads **5 A** and the voltmeter reads **0.75 V**.

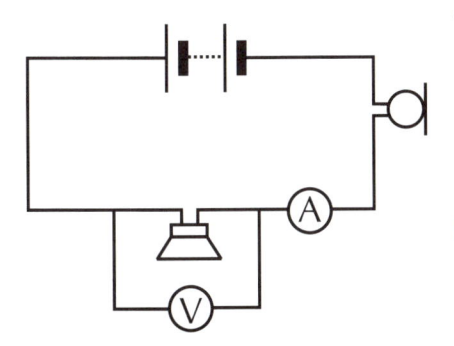

a) Calculate the resistance of the speaker.

....

....

b) Calculate the power of the speaker.

....

....

Q3 Tharindu sets up the circuit in the diagram. The voltmeter reads **9 V**.

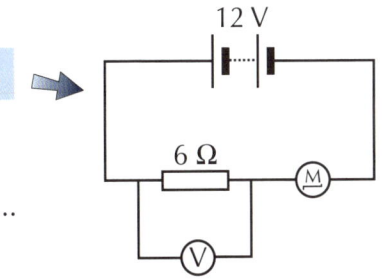

a) What is the **current** flowing through the circuit?

....

b) What is the **voltage** across the motor?

....

c) What is the **resistance** of the motor?

....

Module 5 — Communications

Wireless Communication

Q1 Police officers often use portable two-way radios to talk to each other. Some of the parts of a two-way radio are labelled in the diagram below.

(Diagram: two-way radio with labels — Aerial, Speaker, Tuner, Microphone. Cartoon of two police officers on opposite sides of a wall calling "Officer, come in, where are you?")

a) Draw lines to match up the parts of the radio with their functions.

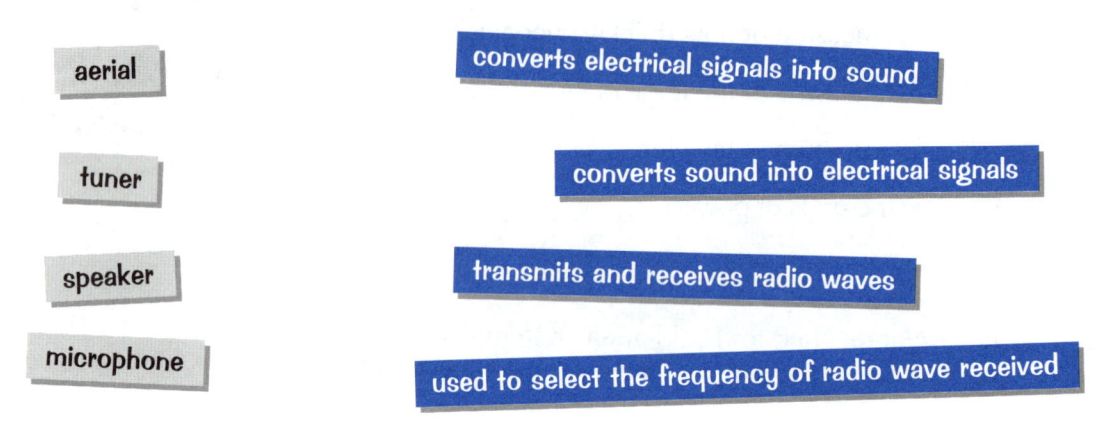

aerial	converts electrical signals into sound
tuner	converts sound into electrical signals
speaker	transmits and receives radio waves
microphone	used to select the frequency of radio wave received

b) Portable radio aerials often consist of a coil of wire wrapped around an iron-rich material. What is this type of aerial called?

....

(Diagram labelled: iron-rich rod, coil of wire)

Q2 Complete the paragraph by choosing words from the box to explain how **radio communication** works.

| amplified | loudspeaker | microphone | demodulator | modulator | tuner |

The .... inside the radio transmitter converts electrical signals into radio waves. The radio waves received at a radio set are converted back into electrical signals by a .... These signals are then .... before a .... converts them into sound.

Top Tips: Wireless communication is everywhere these days — mobile phones, TVs and radios are just a few examples. There are a few tricky details here and there that you need to get to grips with, but we've given you plenty of practice over the next few pages. Dive in and enjoy...

Module 5 — Communications

Wireless Communication

Q3 Katie is a biologist. She uses **radio tracking equipment**, including an aerial like the one shown below, to monitor the movements of animals.

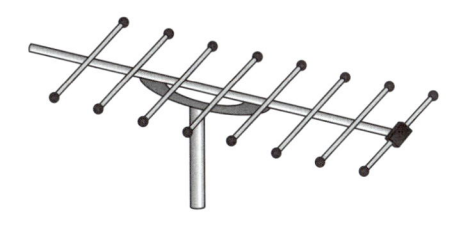

a) Name the type of aerial that Katie is using.

....

b) Give **one** other use for this type of aerial.

....

c) Complete the following sentence by circling the correct angle.

> This type of aerial has **180°** / **360°** reception.

Q4 The picture shows a **'satellite dish farm'**. The dishes are used to receive signals from space.

The diagram below shows how waves reach a detector above the dish.

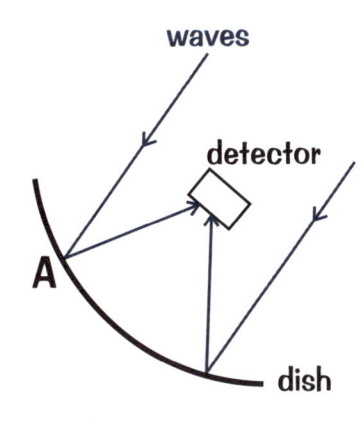

a) What happens to the waves at point A?

....

b) The dishes shown in the picture are used for radio astronomy. Give **one** other use of satellite dishes.

....

Module 5 — Communications

Wireless Communication

Q5 Wireless communications devices use waves to carry **signals**. Different signals are **broadcast** on waves with different **frequencies**.

a) Tick the correct box to show which of the following best describes the frequency of a wave.

☐ Frequency is the distance from one peak to the next.

☐ Frequency is the height from the mid-line to the peak.

☐ Frequency is the number of complete waves there are per second.

b) Complete the table below to show the frequencies used to transmit television, radio and satellite signals. Use words from the list below.

television   satellite   radio

frequency	communication device
100 kHz	
600 MHz	
10 GHz	

Q6 A scientist is comparing diagrams showing four different waves.

A   B

C   D

a) Give the letters of two waves that have the same amplitude. ....

b) Give the letters of two waves that have the same wavelength. ....

Q7 Fatma uses an **oscilloscope** to look at the **input** and **output** waves of an **amplifier**.

A
B

a) Which wave, A or B, is the **input** wave?

....

b) Describe what effect the amplifier has on the input wave.

....

....

Module 5 — Communications

Wireless Communication

Q8 Richard loves listening to his **radio** in his house and in his car when he's driving to work.

a) The diagram below shows how a carrier radio wave is modulated to carry a signal.

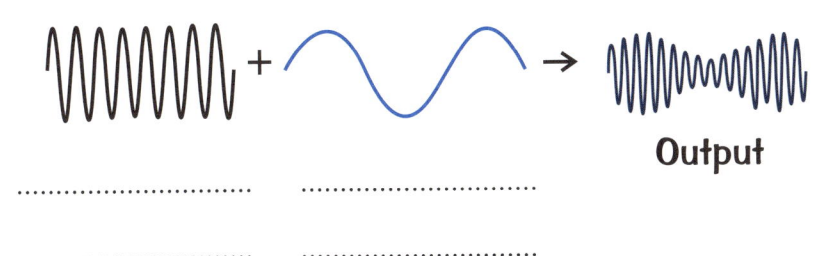

i) On the diagram, label the carrier wave and the signal wave.

ii) Complete the following description of how radio waves carry information.

> The information being sent is called the ....
>
> The radio wave that carries the information is called the ....
>
> The process of putting information into waves is called ....

b) There's a **hill** between Richard's house and the nearest **radio transmitter**, as shown in the diagram. What two things could happen to the radio waves at 'A'?

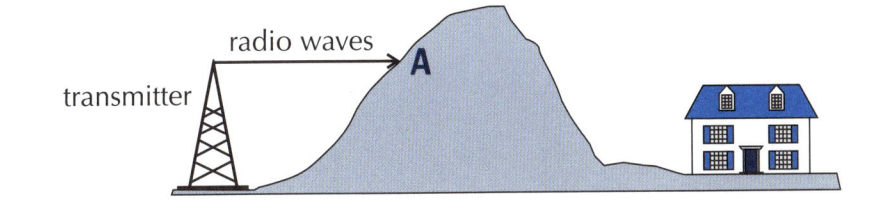

1. ....
2. ....

c) As Richard drives through the city where he works, the radio signal sometimes goes a bit **fuzzy**. This is because the waves bounce off the buildings and take a **different path**, as shown by the diagram below.

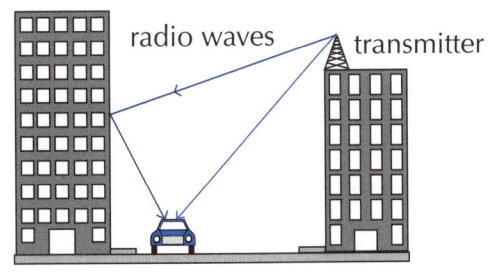

Explain why the signal can become fuzzy when it takes a different path.

....

....

....

Top Tips:
Wireless communication is all about waves — waving at your friends, waving out of the car window. Then there's the trickier details about aerials, modulation, wavelengths, satellite dishes and the rest. There's always something that has to come along and ruin all the fun.

Module 5 — Communications

Analogue and Digital Signals

Q1 Andre is doing his homework. He needs to think of some **advantages** and **disadvantages** of **analogue** and **digital** signals.

Complete the table to show one advantage and one disadvantage for each type of signal.

	Advantage	Disadvantage
Analogue		
Digital		

Q2 An electrical appliance shop sells **digital set top boxes**, which enable people to watch **digitally broadcast** programmes on an **analogue** television.

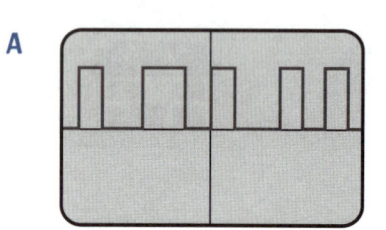

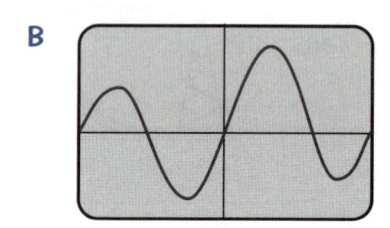

A   B

a) Which diagram, A or B, represents an analogue signal? ....

b) Use words from the box to complete the passage describing analogue and digital signals.

| variable | fixed | discrete | continuous |

An analogue signal is .... and ....
A digital signal has .... and .... values.

c) Give one reason why the **picture quality** on a television **improves** after installing a set top box.

....
....

Module 5 — Communications

Converting Analogue to Digital

Q1 Digital signals are created using **sampling**.

a) i) Complete the diagram below to show how an analogue signal is sampled.

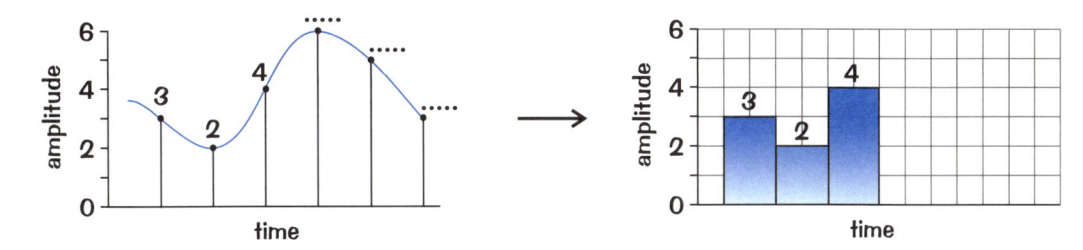

ii) Digital numbers are changed into a code to form a digital signal.
Use the table below to write the code produced by the analogue signal above.

Number	0	1	2	3	4	5	6	7	8
Binary code	0000	0001	0010	0011	0100	0101	0110	0111	1000

....

b) Another digital signal is shown on the right.

1 1 0 1 1 0 1 0 1 0 1 0 0 0 1 1 0

i) circle one **bit** of data and label it 'bit'.

ii) circle one **byte** of data and label it 'byte'.

Q2 Martin has a large collection of music on **vinyl records**. He has bought some computer software that will enable him to **record** the music onto his **computer** and store it as **digital data**.

The software gives Martin a choice of sampling rates he can use to convert the music.

a) Explain what is meant by sampling rate.

....

b) Which of the sampling rates on the right should Martin use to record his music at the best possible quality?   **20 kHz**   **30 kHz**   **40 kHz**
Circle the correct answer.

Q3 Graham is buying a book from a website and is asked to send his **credit card** information over the **internet**. He is told that the information will be **encrypted**.

a) Why is it important that credit card information sent over the internet is encrypted?

....

....

b) Give one other example of a signal encrypted for security.

....

Module 5 — Communications

Converting Analogue to Digital

Q4 Marcia is comparing the **bit rates** of different **modems**.

Modem	Bit rate (bits per second)
A	56 000
B	14 000
C	9 600
D	33 600

a) Explain what is meant by bit rate.

....

b) Which modem will have the **fastest** connection speed?

....

c) Calculate how many **bytes** of information modem A will process in one second.

....

Q5 The United Kingdom is currently in the process of switching **television broadcasting** from **analogue to digital**. There are **costs** and **benefits** associated with the switchover.

a) Suggest one **cost** to consumers of the switchover.

....

....

b) Suggest one **benefit** to consumers of the switchover.

....

....

c) Explain why digital communication becomes more cost-effective the more it is used.

....

....

Top Tips: Sampling — well I'll try a bit of that chocolate one. And perhaps some of the strawberry one too. Oh — you mean converting from analogue to digital signals... my mistake.

Module 5 — Communications

Communication Links

Q1 **Communication links** carry information between communications devices.

a) Match up the types of communication link with how the information is carried.

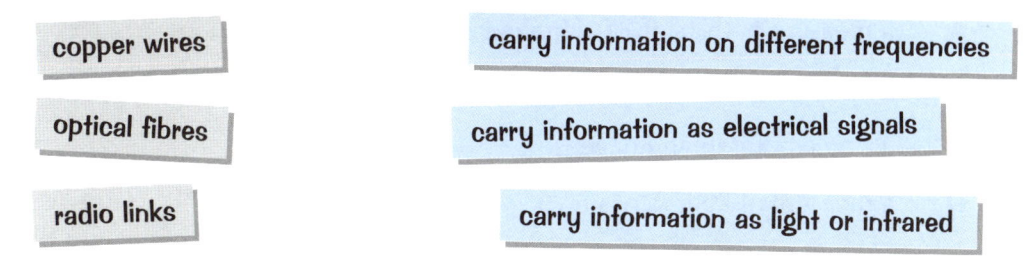

copper wires	carry information on different frequencies
optical fibres	carry information as electrical signals
radio links	carry information as light or infrared

b) Give an example of a communications system that uses radio links.

....

Q2 Sarah draws a block diagram of a landline **telephone communication system**.

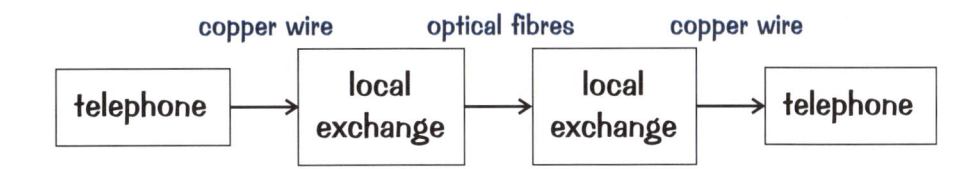

telephone → [copper wire] → local exchange → [optical fibres] → local exchange → [copper wire] → telephone

a) i) Circle the type of signal that the **copper wires** are likely to carry. digital / **analogue**

ii) Suggest one reason why copper wires are chosen to link the telephones to the exchange.

....

b) **Optical fibres** are used between the telephone exchanges.

i) Circle the type of information that this link is likely to carry. **digital** / analogue

ii) Give two reasons why optical fibres are used instead of copper wires.

1. ....

2. ....

iii) Suggest one other use for optical fibres.

....

c) Sarah prefers to communicate with her friends by **email** rather than by telephone.
Give two examples of a portable device that she could use to store data received by email.

1. ....

2. ....

Module 5 — Communications

Pictures and Video

Q1 Kevin has just bought a **3.1 megapixel digital camera**.

a) What is a pixel? Circle the correct letter from the list below.

- A   a measure of the size of an image
- B   a bit of data
- C   a single point in an image
- D   a measure of light intensity

b) Kevin can store his photos as 'GIF' files or as 'TIFF' files. GIF files store images using 8 bpp (bits per pixel), and TIFF files store images using up to 48 bpp. How does the bpp affect the photo image?

....

Q2 A tourist takes some **video footage** using two different settings on her camera. Some information about the footage she has taken is shown in the table below.

	pixel word size (bits)	pixels per frame	refresh rate
setting A	8	400 000	24
setting B	1	1 700 000	24

a) What is meant by a **frame**?

....

b) What units is the **refresh rate** measured in? Circle the correct letter from the list below.

- A   metres per second
- B   pixels per minute
- C   frames per second
- D   pixels per frame

c) i) Explain what video **bit rate** is.

....

ii) Calculate the video bit rate for Setting A.

....

....

Top Tips: So that's another section over. Well, all but the mixed questions. And what useful things they are. The topics are likely to be all mixed up in the exam, and practice makes perfect...

Module 5 — Communications

Mixed Questions for Module 5

Q1 Nathan is an **aerial engineer**. He installs aerials in homes and factories.

a) Suggest one technical skill that Nathan needs for his job.

....

b) Nathan often installs dish-shaped aerials. Give one use for this type of aerial.

....

Q2 A student sends a **text message** to a friend. A block diagram of the process is shown below.

mobile phone → base station → base station → mobile phone

a) What do the arrows in the block diagram represent?

....

b) What is the **input** device shown in the block diagram? ....

c) Before the information is sent, it is **encrypted**. Explain why.

....

d) The information is sent as a signal on a **microwave**. Which of the following is the most likely frequency of this microwave? Circle the correct answer below.

    1 Hz   100 MHz   100 kHz   10 GHz

Q3 Millie buys a camera with an **automatic flash**.

a) Which of the following electrical components will the camera contain, so that the flash will automatically be used in low levels of light? Circle the correct answer.

    variable resistor   light-emitting diode   photodiode   thermistor

b) Millie takes a picture with her new camera and transfers it to her computer. The size of the picture is **160 000 bytes**.

    i) How many **bits** are in Millie's picture?

....

    ii) Millie emails the picture to a friend. The bit rate of her modem is **56 000 bits per second**. How long will it take to transmit the picture?

....

Module 5 — Communications

Mixed Questions for Module 5

Q4 Chris has just finished installing some new **lights** in his kitchen.
The **circuit diagram** of his new **low-voltage** lighting circuit is shown below.

a) What is represented by **A**?

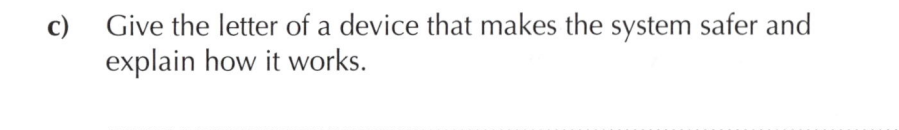

....

b) Describe the function of **device C**.

....

c) Give the letter of a device that makes the system safer and explain how it works.

....

....

Q5 The **product specifications** of two different **CCTV cameras** are shown below.

Feature	Camera A	Camera B
Power source	Battery, mains	Battery
Operating voltage	12 V	12 V
Maximum voltage	13 V	13 V
Operating current	0.4 A	0.4 A
Pixels per frame	300 000	200 000
Pixel word size	4 bits per pixel	1 bits per pixel
Refresh rate	10 frames per sec	5 frames per sec

a) Which camera will produce the **most detailed** video footage? Give a reason for your answer.

....

....

b) Camera A can be powered using the mains or a battery. Give one advantage of using:

i) battery power ....

ii) mains power ....

c) Calculate the operating power of Camera A.

....

d) The video footage can be transferred to a computer. The speed of this transfer depends on the video bit rate. Calculate the video bit rate for Camera B.

....

Module 5 — Communications

Mixed Questions for Module 5

Q6 Tim sets up a series circuit containing a **battery**, an **ammeter**, **two lamps**, a **light-emitting diode** and a **thermistor**.

a) Draw Tim's circuit in the box.

b) Complete the following sentence about the circuit by using the words below.

| voltage | current |

The .... is the same at every point in the circuit but the .... is shared between the components.

c) When the voltage across the light-emitting diode is 1.0 V, it has a resistance of 5 Ω. Calculate the **current** flowing through the light-emitting diode.

....

Q7 A **telecommunications engineer** is testing a radio communications system.

a) One of the cables attached to the radio transmitter aerial has this symbol on it. What does the symbol mean?

....

b) Part of the block diagram for the radio communications system is shown on the right.

microphone → modulator → transmitter aerial

Describe the function of the modulator.

....

c) The engineer finds that there is a large amount of **interference** in the radio signals received at a nearby receiver aerial. What is interference?

....

....

d) The invention of radios has made it easier to communicate over long distances. Name another electronic device that has increased the distance of human communication.

....

Top Tips: If, like me, you found that as much fun as scooping out your eyes with a dirty spoon, then you'll be glad to hear that it's the last page of this section... wooooo hooooo...

Module 5 — Communications

Selecting Materials

Q1 Darren works for a film production company as a **set designer**. He needs to know a lot about different **materials** and their **properties**. Give **two** other examples of jobs for which knowledge of materials and their properties is needed.

1. ....

2. ....

Q2 'The Helmet Shack' are trying to develop a new **cycle helmet**. The designers have produced a list of **desirable properties** that the helmet should have.

Draw lines to match the properties to the correct criteria. One has been done for you.

The helmet needs to be very hard-wearing

The helmet needs to look attractive

The helmet needs to be quite cheap — Cost

The helmet needs to be made using methods that produce as little pollution as possible

Aesthetic appeal

Cost

Environmental impact

Durability

Q3 The table below gives information about different methods for **joining** materials.

Method	Used to join	Strength of join
Crimping	metal-metal	average
Riveting	metal-metal	very strong
Glue A	wood-wood	strong
Glue B	plastic-wood	strong

We are gathered here to join these two metals in holy matrimony...

Which of these methods would you use to attach:

a) The metal wings of a plane to the metal body? Give a reason for your answer.

....

b) The legs to the seat of a wooden chair? Give a reason for your answer.

....

c) A plastic coat hook to the back of a door? Give a reason for your answer.

....

Health and Safety

Q1 Shazma is a **trading standards officer**. She has written a leaflet explaining why **product standards** are important.

Complete the following extract from Shazma's leaflet using words from the list below.

> injury   tested   quality   fire   safe   consistently

When people buy products they want to be sure the products are

.... If a product conforms to a particular standard, it will have

been .... thoroughly, for example to make sure that it doesn't

cause .... and won't catch .... under

normal use. Standards also ensure that the products are .... of

a high ....

Q2 The diagram below shows a sticker that Henry found on the back of his **stereo**.

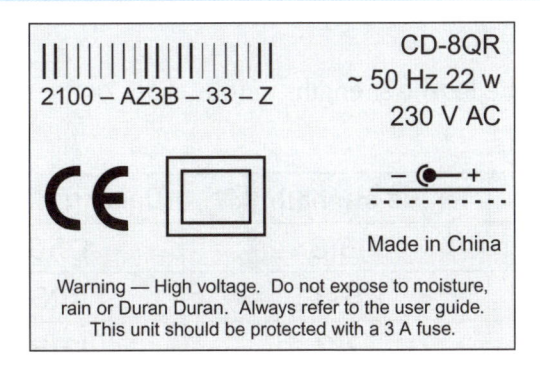

```
||||||||||||||          CD-8QR
2100 – AZ3B – 33 – Z   ~ 50 Hz 22 w
                        230 V AC

   CE    [ ]           – (•– +

                       Made in China
Warning — High voltage. Do not expose to moisture,
rain or Duran Duran. Always refer to the user guide.
This unit should be protected with a 3 A fuse.
```

a) Draw a circle around the mark which shows that the stereo conforms to a set of quality and safety standards.

b) Which standards organisation has certified this stereo? Circle the correct answer.

British Standards Institution   European Committee for Standardisation   International Organisation for Standards

Q3 Ludwig is a **civil engineer**. He is working on the design for a new **skyscraper**. When he designs structures like skyscrapers he has to include a large **safety margin**.

Give two other examples of things that are designed with a large safety margin.

....

....

Module 6 — Materials and Performance

Mechanical Properties

Q1 Circle the correct word in each pair to show whether the following diagrams show objects under **compression** or **tension**.

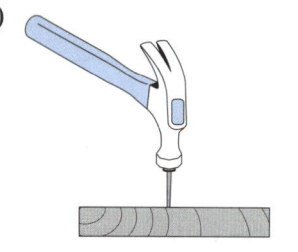

a) The cable is under

tension / compression.

b) The nail is under

tension / compression.

c) The suitcase hinges are under

tension / compression.

The clothes inside it are under

tension / compression.

Q2 Pablo works for a company that makes **climbing ropes**. He's investigating the **mechanical properties** of some different **materials** including their **tensile strength**.

a) What is meant by tensile strength?

....

The table below shows the tensile strengths of four ropes of the same thickness made from different materials.

Rope	Tensile strength (kN)	Density (kg/m³)
A	15.3	1750
B	5.8	1120
C	7.3	1318
D	10.1	1158

b) i) Which rope has the **greatest** tensile strength?

....

ii) Suggest why this rope might not be suitable for use as a climbing rope.

....

....

iii) Other than tensile strength and density, suggest **one** other mechanical property that Pablo should investigate. Explain why this property is important for climbing ropes.

....

....

Module 6 — Materials and Performance

Mechanical Properties

Q3 Draw lines to connect each **mechanical property** with the correct **definition**.

Flexibility — a material's resistance to scratching and indentation

Density — how easily a material's shape can be changed

Hardness — how much mass there is in a given volume

Q4 Kelly works for a company that designs **pole vault poles**. The materials used to make the poles have to have certain **properties**.

a) Kelly says that the **density** of the material needs to be as low as possible. Explain why.

....

b) The pole needs to bend and straighten many times without breaking. What mechanical property should the material have in order to satisfy this requirement?

....

Q5 Sam is a **bowl designer** — she designs bowls for a supermarket chain. Some of the bowls she designs are for **adults** and some are for **small children**.

Bowl for small children — made from plastic

Bowl for adults — made from ceramic material

a) Suggest why ceramics are suitable for making bowls for adults.

....

b) Why shouldn't a ceramic material be used to make bowls for small children?

....

....

Module 6 — Materials and Performance

Measuring Properties

Q1 For his science coursework Hugo wanted to investigate the **stiffness** of three different materials.

a) In the space below draw a labelled diagram of the apparatus that Hugo could use to measure the stiffness of the different materials.

b) Hugo made sure that all the samples he used were the **same thickness**.
Why did he need to do this?

....

c) A graph of Hugo's results is shown below.

Which material had the lowest stiffness?

....

d) Describe how Hugo could measure the **tensile strength** of each sample of material.

....

....

Module 6 — Materials and Performance

Measuring Properties

Q2 Miriam works in the **quality assurance department** of a company that makes **trampolines**. She is testing the **compressive strength** of the leg of an indoor trampoline, using the apparatus shown below.

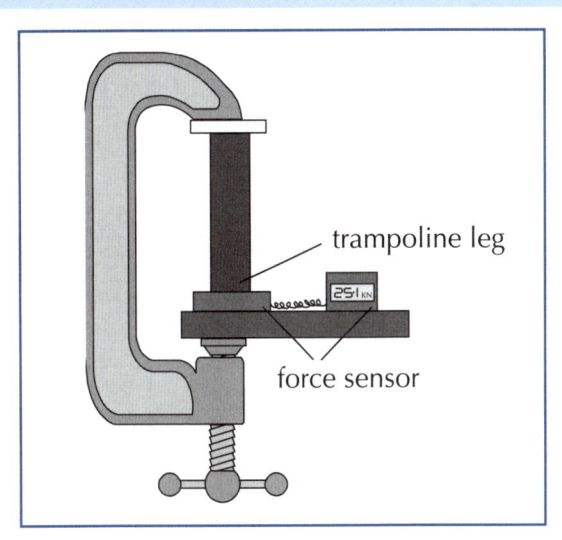

a) Suggest **two** safety precautions that Miriam should take when doing this experiment.

1. ....

2. ....

b) Miriam found that the compressive strength of the leg was 1010 N. Briefly describe how Miriam will have used the apparatus shown above to get this result.

....

....

....

c) To pass the quality tests the leg has to withstand a force of 1000 N or greater. Miriam recorded that this leg reached the standard required. Explain why Miriam should test many more trampoline legs.

....

....

Top Tips: It's dead important that you don't get your compressive and tensile strengths muddled up. They're two completely different things and they're measured in two different ways. Make sure you can describe the methods (and draw the apparatus) for measuring both.

Module 6 — Materials and Performance

Interpreting Data

Q1 Wendy is testing **concrete pillars** that can be used to build a **bridge**. She measures how a concrete pillar compresses under different loads. The loads are measured in **kN** and the compressions in **mm**. Wendy's results are shown in the table below.

Load	Compression		
	Pillar 1	Pillar 2	Average
0	0.0	0.0	
100	0.1	0.3	
200	0.4	0.4	
300	0.7	0.5	
400	0.8	1.2	
500	1.0	1.0	
600	1.2	1.2	
700	1.3	1.5	
800	1.6	1.6	

a) What is wrong with the top row of Wendy's table?

....

b) Complete the right hand column of the table by working out the average compression for each load.

Average = total of the results / number of results

c) Plot a graph of the data on the grid opposite and draw a line of best fit. (Remember to label the axes.)

d) What conclusions can be drawn from these results?

....

....

....

e) Draw a ring around any results that are outliers.

f) Suggest **one** thing Wendy would need to keep constant to make it a fair test.

....

....

Module 6 — Materials and Performance

Elastic and Plastic Behaviour

Q1 As part of his job, Guppi is making leaflets explaining the difference between **elastic** and **plastic** behaviour, to send out with samples of different products.

Use words from the box below to complete the passage to help Guppi write an introduction to his leaflet. Each word can be used once, more than once or not at all.

| shape | elastically | force | plastically |

The words 'elastic' and 'plastic' are often used to describe how materials behave, not just what they're made from. A material that behaves .... will return to its original .... once the .... is removed. A material that behaves .... won't return to its original shape.

Usually, materials behave .... for small loads and .... for large loads.

Q2 Circle the **correct** word in each pair to show whether the materials in the following diagrams are behaving **elastically** or **plastically**.

a) Car bodywork deforms **plastically / elastically** during a crash.

b) The cushions of the settee are behaving **plastically / elastically**.

c) Bungee cords deform **plastically / elastically** during a jump.

d) Wooden blocks deform **plastically / elastically** when they are karate chopped.

Module 6 — Materials and Performance

Elastic and Plastic Behaviour

Q3 Oscar works for the **British Standards Institution**. He is testing some **springs** on a children's toy before it is given a BSI kitemark. He has plotted a **force-extension graph** for one of the springs.

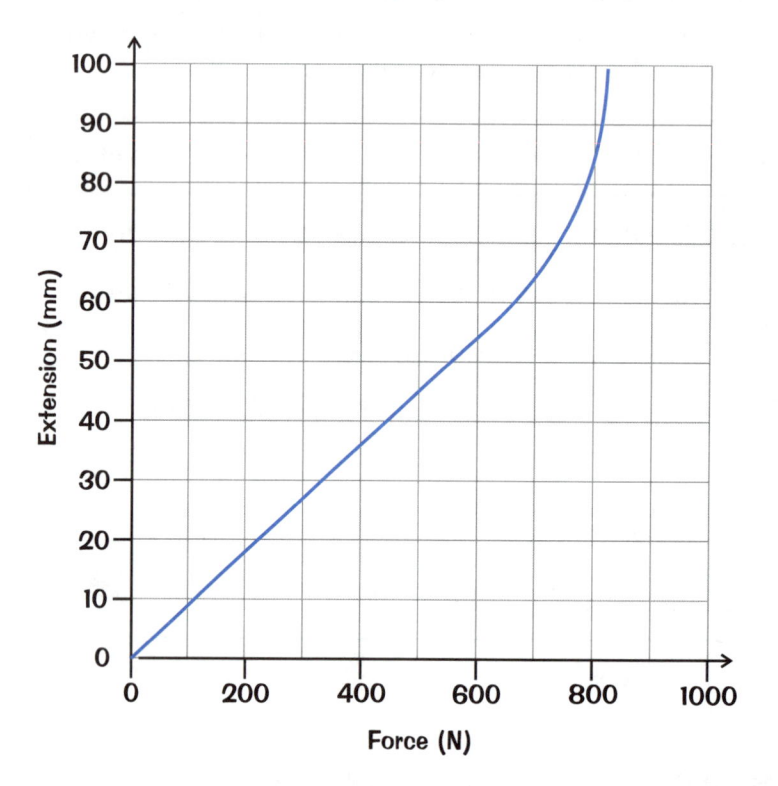

a) To pass the standards test, the spring must extend by more than **42 mm** when a force of **500 N** is applied.

   i) What is the extension of the spring when a force of 500 N is applied?

   ....

   ii) Does the spring pass the test? ....

b) The standard also says that the spring's elastic limit cannot be less than **900 N**.

   i) What is meant by the term **elastic limit**?

   ....

   ....

   ii) What is the elastic limit of the spring being tested? ....

   iii) What would happen to the spring if a force of **800 N** was applied?

   ....

Top Tips:
Remember, things don't have to be made out of plastic or elastic to behave plastically or elastically — it's just a way of describing how materials behave. Make sure you can use a graph like the one above to tell when an object is behaving plastically or elastically.

Module 6 — Materials and Performance

Metals, Ceramics and Polymers

Q1 After building some **furniture**, Simon has a big pile of different materials on his workshop bench. He decides to **organise** all the materials into different **classes**.

a) Complete the labels on the drawers of Simon's materials cabinet to show the five main classes of materials. The first one has been done for you.

b) Simon's leftover materials are given in the list below. Draw lines to show which materials belong in which classes. One has been done for you.

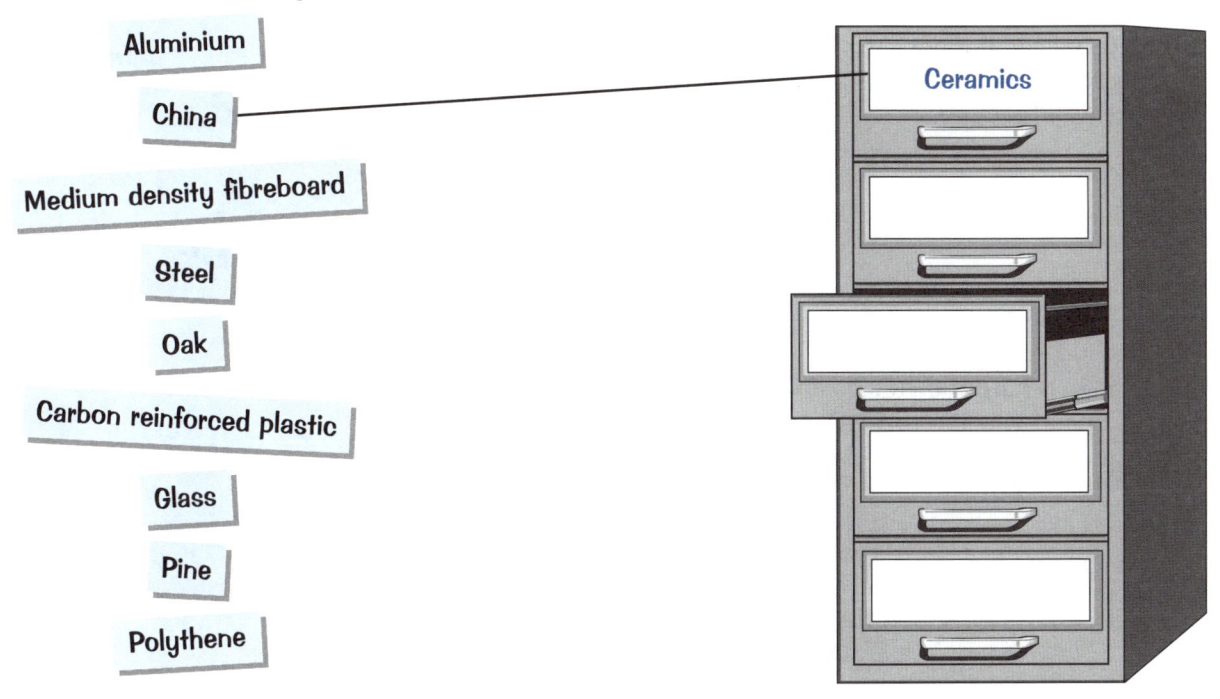

- Aluminium
- China
- Medium density fibreboard
- Steel
- Oak
- Carbon reinforced plastic
- Glass
- Pine
- Polythene

(Drawer labelled: Ceramics)

Q2 Melanie wants to separate some metals, ceramics and polymers based on their **physical properties**.

a) After some research, she finds out that ceramics are **brittle**.

  i) Explain what is meant by brittle.

  ....

  ii) Other than being brittle, state **two** other physical properties of ceramics.

  ....

  ....

b) Melanie has written descriptions of two materials. Say what types of material A and B are.

> Material A is a good conductor of electricity and heat. It is shiny and stiff and can be drawn into wires.

> Material B is a good insulator of electricity and heat. It is flexible and doesn't return to its original shape if you stretch it.

Material A is ....

Material B is ....

Module 6 — Materials and Performance

Alloys and Composites

Q1 Su-lin works for a **steel manufacturing company**. She is investigating the properties of different types of steel. Steel is made up of **iron** and a small amount of **carbon**.

a) Steel is a metal alloy. What is meant by the term alloy? Circle the correct answer.

   solid composite   solid solution   aqueous solution   acidic solution

b) The diagram opposite shows the iron atoms in steel. Complete the diagram by drawing in the carbon atoms.

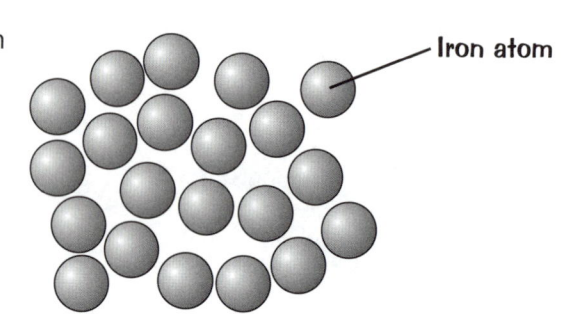

c) Steel is **harder** than iron and has a **higher tensile strength**. Explain why this makes steel better than iron for making:

   i) chisels for carving wood,

   ....

   ii) cables for supporting buildings.

   ....

d) Give **one** other way, apart from hardness and tensile strength, in which the properties of alloys often differ from those of pure metals.

   ....

Q2 A **sports shop** sells some equipment that is made from **composite materials**.

a) What are composite materials?

   ....
   ....

b) Give one use of composite materials in sports equipment.

   ....

c) State one use of composite materials other than in sports equipment.

   ....

Module 6 — Materials and Performance

Materials and Forces

Q1 Geoff works as a designer for the Damota car company. He needs a very good understanding of **velocity**, **momentum** and **forces**.

   a) Geoff is explaining to his apprentice that speed and velocity are different. What is velocity?

   ....

   ....

   b) Describe the relationship between momentum, mass and velocity.

   ....

   ....

   c) Geoff is working on the designs for the 'Tiny' (a really small car) and the 'Guzzler' (a massive sports car). The Guzzler has **more mass** than the Tiny.

   i) If both cars were travelling at the same speed, which car would have the **larger momentum**?

   ....

   ii) How could Geoff make both cars have the same momentum?

   ....

   d) Which factors affect the momentum of an object? Circle the correct answer(s).

   shape   mass   hardness   speed   potential energy   direction   temperature

Q2 An **automotive safety specialist** is investigating the **brakes** of a car.

   a) What happens to momentum of a car when the brakes are applied?

   ....

   b) The car below is braking. Draw an arrow showing the direction of the braking force.

   ← Original velocity

Module 6 — Materials and Performance

Materials and Forces

Q3 Hardeep is investigating the effectiveness of **air bags**. He crashes two identical cars into a wall at **10 m/s**. Only one of the cars is fitted with an air bag. Hardeep measures the **forces** acting on crash test dummies in the cars as they crash into the wall.

a) The dummies each have a mass of 80 kg. Use the equation **momentum = mass × velocity** to calculate a dummy's momentum before it crashes into the wall.

....

b) Hardeep uses the formula **change in momentum = force × time** to study the action of the air bag. First he measures the car without an air bag. His results are shown below.

	Without an air bag	With an air bag
Change in dummy's momentum	800 kgm/s	.... 800 kgm/s
Time taken for dummy to stop	0.1 s	.... 0.1 s
Force acting on dummy	8000 N	.... 8000 N

Hardeep then measures these quantities for the dummy in the car with the air bag. Use the following words to complete the table above.

      higher than   **less than**   **the same as**

c) Use the information in the table to help explain how air bags improve road safety.

....

....

d) Give **two** examples of other devices that improve road safety based on the same principles as air bags.

....

....

e) Suggest **two** examples of materials used in road safety devices, and explain how they work.

....

....

....

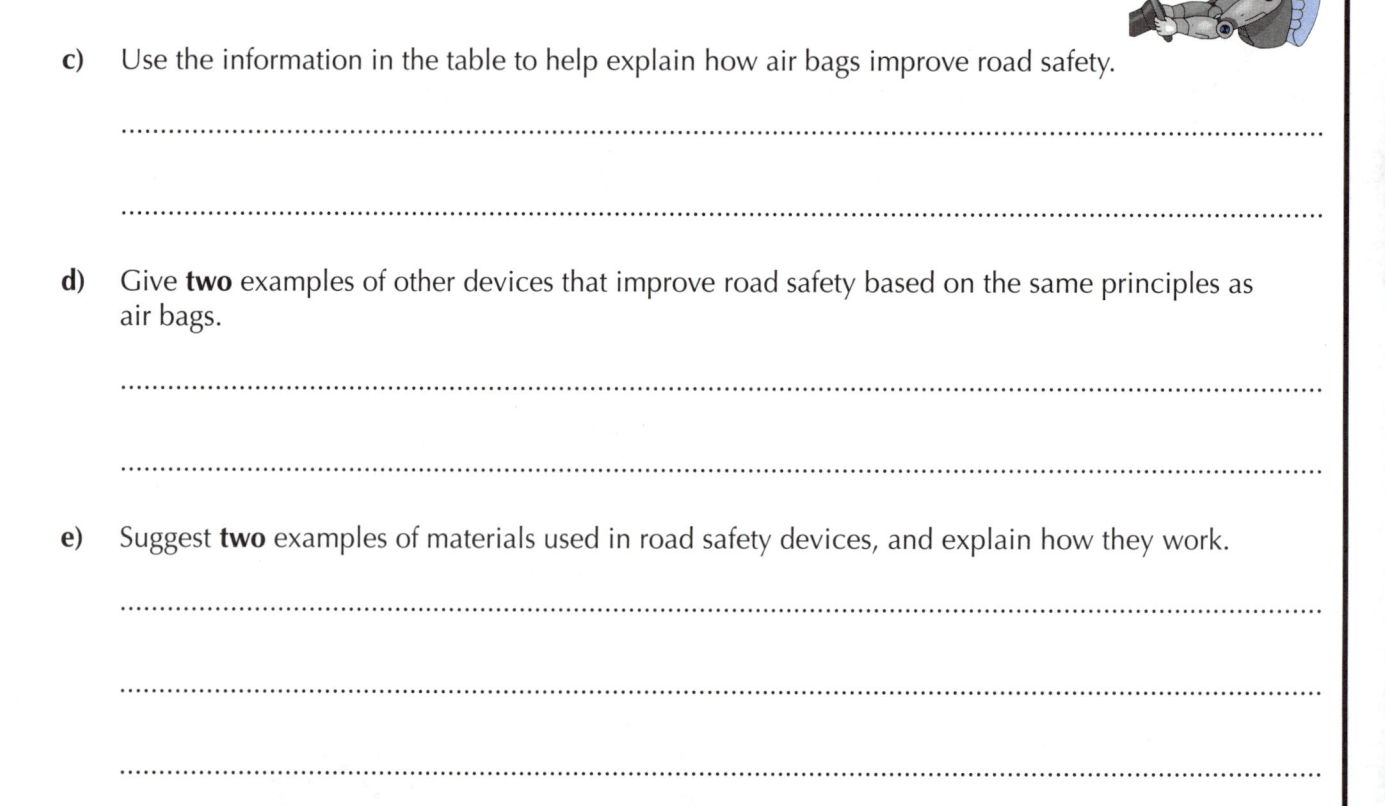

Top Tips: Materials and forces may seem like a bit of an odd thing to follow on from materials and their properties but it's all linked together. With things like car safety devices, you need to know about the properties of materials used to make them to understand how they work.

Module 6 — Materials and Performance

Electrical and Thermal Properties

Q1 Amy is designing a new type of **spotlight** for her local theatre. She needs to find a material which has **high electrical conductance** but **low thermal expansion**.

   a) Describe the meaning of:

      i) electrical conductance ....

      ....

      ii) thermal expansion ....

      ....

Amy has found two materials that are both good electrical conductors.
She wants to measure the **thermal expansion** of each material.

   b) In the space below, draw a labelled diagram of some apparatus Amy could use to measure the thermal expansion of the materials.

   c) The diagram below shows the materials used to make the electrical cable for the spotlight.

Explain why:

      i) copper is a suitable material for the wiring inside the cable.

      ....

      ii) plastic is a suitable material for the outer layers of the cable.

      ....

Module 6 — Materials and Performance

Electrical and Thermal Properties

Q2 Dave is designing an office. He needs to choose materials for the buildings and fittings. Some of the materials should be **good thermal conductors** and some should be **poor thermal conductors**.

a) On the labels below write 'G' where Dave needs a **good thermal conductor** and write 'P' where Dave needs to use a **poor thermal conductor**.

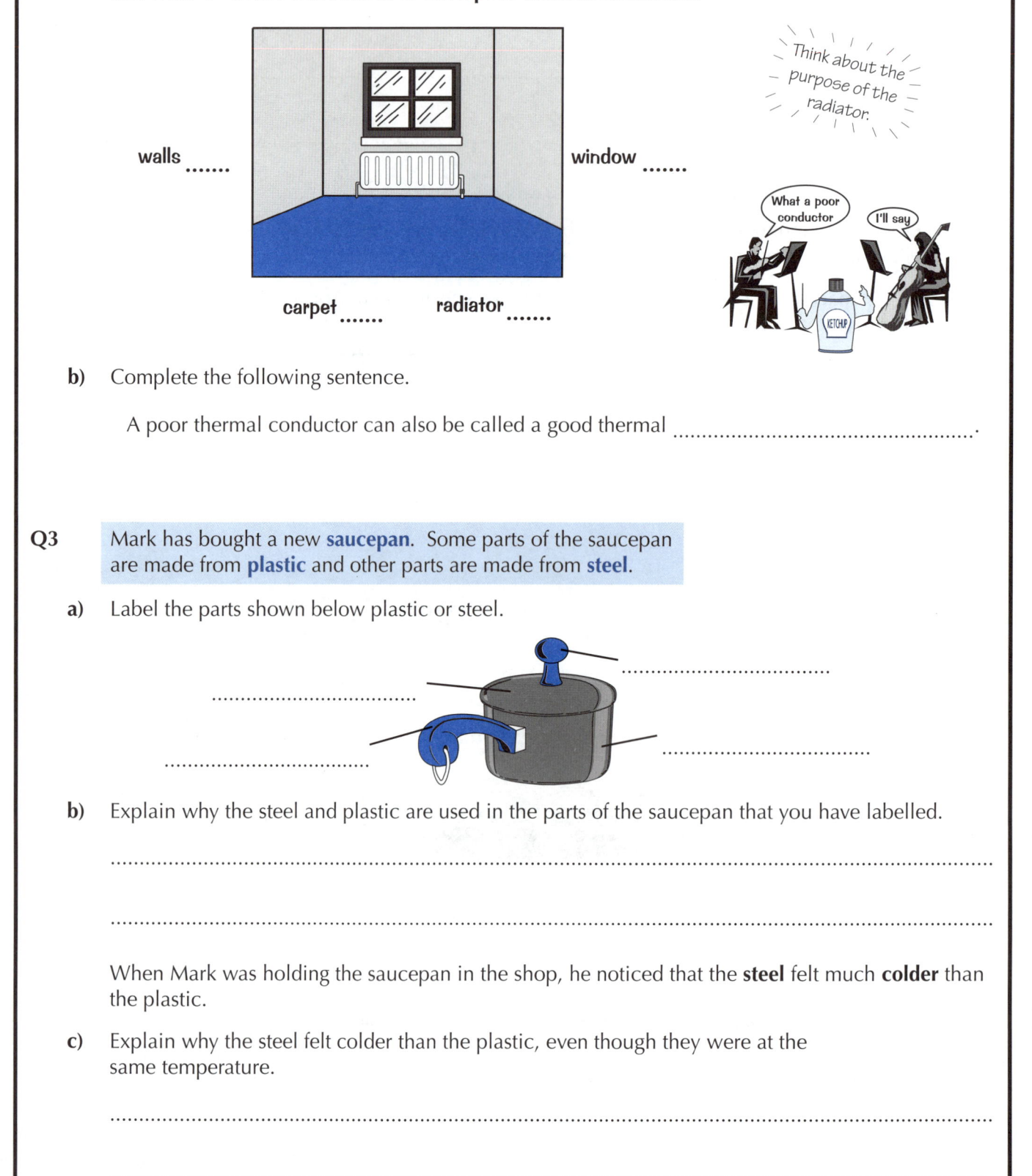

walls ....   window ....   carpet ....   radiator ....

b) Complete the following sentence.

A poor thermal conductor can also be called a good thermal ....

Q3 Mark has bought a new **saucepan**. Some parts of the saucepan are made from **plastic** and other parts are made from **steel**.

a) Label the parts shown below plastic or steel.

b) Explain why the steel and plastic are used in the parts of the saucepan that you have labelled.

....

....

When Mark was holding the saucepan in the shop, he noticed that the **steel** felt much **colder** than the plastic.

c) Explain why the steel felt colder than the plastic, even though they were at the same temperature.

....

....

Module 6 — Materials and Performance

Acoustic Properties

Q1 Kobe designs **synthesizers** for a living. He is testing a new signal generator. He connects the signal generator to a **loudspeaker** to see what sound it makes.

Kobe can adjust the **frequency** and **amplitude** of the sound waves using the signal generator.

a) Circle the correct word in each pair to complete the sentences below.

   i) The number of vibrations per second is the **frequency** / amplitude of a wave.

   ii) The size of the vibrations is the frequency / **amplitude** of a wave.

b) Kobe **increased** the frequency by turning the dial on the signal generator. How did the sound change?

....

c) How could Kobe adjust the properties of the sound waves to make the sound **quieter**?

....

Q2 A **musician** buys a **synthesizer** to use with her **keyboard**.

Complete the paragraph below using the words provided. Words can be used once, more than once or not at all.

frequencies   louder   3000 Hz   amplitude   decibels   2000 Hz   vibrations   quieter

The musician notices that notes with .... of about 2000 Hz sounded much .... than other notes, even though the amplitude of the .... was the same. This is because the human ear is more sensitive to some .... and is most sensitive at .... This means that sounds at this frequency seem .... than other frequencies with the same ....

Module 6 — Materials and Performance

Acoustic Properties

Q3 John is an **environmental health practitioner**. He has written a leaflet about noise and the **decibel (dB) scale**.

a) Fill in the blanks using the correct numbers from below. Numbers can be used once or not at all.

| 60 | 85 | 20 | 40 | 10 | 130 | 105 |

Normal conversations occur at about .... dB. To double the loudness you have to increase the intensity by .... dB. Sound intensities above .... dB can cause temporary hearing loss and intensities above .... dB cause pain.

The leaflet recommends that people wear ear protection if they are exposed to loud noise for a long time.

b) List **two** problems that people could suffer from if they don't follow this advice.

1. ....

2. ....

Q4 An **acoustic engineer** has a piece of equipment which measures the intensity of sound on the **decibel scale**. He thinks that this equipment might be broken. He decides to test the equipment by measuring sounds of known **intensities**.

He plots the following graph.

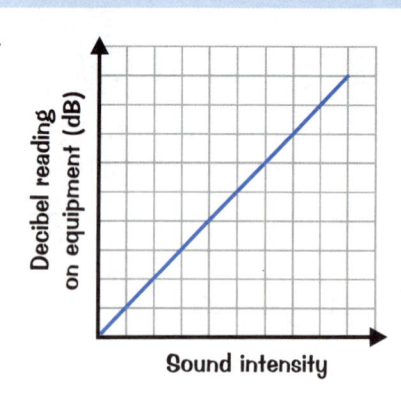

a) Is the equipment working properly? Tick the box to show which statement is correct.

Yes — the graph shows a linear relationship. ☐

No — the graph shows a linear relationship. ☐

b) Circle the correct word(s) to complete the following sentence.

On the decibel scale, an increase in intensity of 20 dB

means the sound will be **twice** / **four times** as loud.

Module 6 — Materials and Performance

Acoustic Properties

Q5 Rachel is an **environmental health officer**. She visits Pauline, who lives near a textile factory. Pauline has complained that the factory is making too much noise. Rachel measures the **noise levels** in Pauline's house when the factory is in operation and when the machinery is switched off.

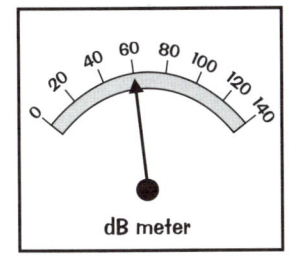

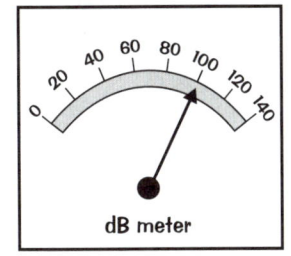

a) How many times louder is the noise in Pauline's house when the factory machinery is switched on?

....

Machinery off   Machinery on

Rachel recommends that Pauline alters some of the materials inside and outside her house, to reduce noise levels inside.

b) Circle the correct word in each pair to complete the sentence below.

> To reduce noise levels in Pauline's house she needs materials that
>
> **absorb** / **reflect** noise generated inside and **transmit** / **reflect** sounds made outside.

c) Describe **one** thing that Pauline could do to her house to reduce the noise coming from outside.

....

Rachel then visits the textile factory. She finds that the noise level is dangerously high. She orders the factory to reduce the noise level by isolating the vibrations from the machines.

d) Suggest **two** methods the factory could use to isolate the vibrations.

1. ....

2. ....

Q6 'The Ledge' plays drums for a local rock band. He practises in his **bedroom**. His neighbours have complained about the **noise**.

Suggest two ways 'The Ledge' could alter his bedroom to reduce the noise level outside.

1. ....

2. ....

Top Tips: Reducing noise is all about putting the right materials in the right places. In some places you need materials that absorb sound. In others you need to reflect sound — make sure you get it the right way round. Think about exam halls and why teachers in clicky heels make such a racket...

Module 6 — Materials and Performance

Optical Properties

Q1 Ahmed works in a toy shop. He is sorting marbles into bags, based on their **optical properties**.

a) Draw lines to show which marble should go into which bag.

| Reflective | Opaque | Transparent | Translucent |

No light passes through this marble.

You can see clearly through this marble.

Light can get through but you can't see clearly through this marble.

You can see your face in this marble.

b) Ahmed notices that a ray of light refracts when it enters the transparent marble. Explain what is meant by **refraction**.

....

....

Q2 June makes **mirrors** for a living. She makes a basic mirror by coating a sheet of **glass** with a thin layer of reflective aluminium. She then protects the back of the mirror with a piece of wood.

a) Circle the **two** properties of glass that make it useful for mirrors.

soft   transparent   hard   reflective

b) Give two examples of the use of mirrors.

1. ....

2. ....

The glassware company that June buys her glass from also produces specialised glass.

c) Name two types of specialised glass and give an example of how each might be used.

1. ....

2. ....

Module 6 — Materials and Performance

Lenses

Q1 Harry is an **optician**. He needs some **weak converging** lenses for a pair of glasses.

a) All of the lenses are made from the same type of glass. Which lens should Harry choose? Circle the correct answer.

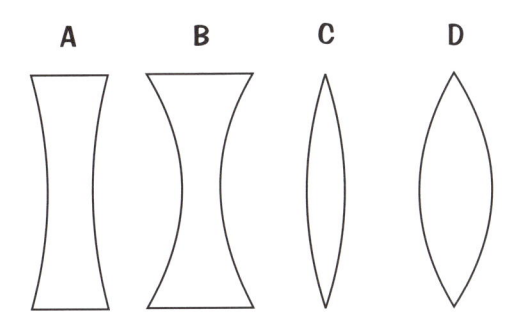

A   B   C   D

b) For the other three lenses, state whether they are weak or strong and whether they are converging or diverging.

Lens .... is **strong** / **weak** and **converging** / **diverging**.

Lens .... is **strong** / **weak** and **converging** / **diverging**.

Lens .... is **strong** / **weak** and **converging** / **diverging**.

Q2 A **scientist** is testing some lenses. He projects some **rays** from a far off point through a **lens**.

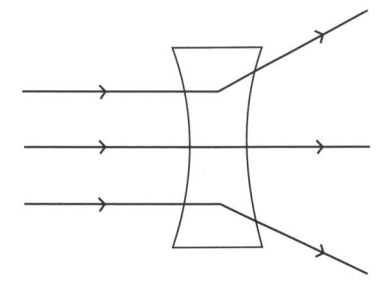

a) The rays coming out of the lens seem to come from a point close by. Mark with an 'X' the point where the rays seem to come from.

b) The scientist places the lens in a frame to make a **magnifying glass**. What sort of image does a magnifying glass produce? Circle the correct answer.

real image   virtual image

Top Tips: Both types of lens bend light rays — it's just how they bend them that differs. Converging lenses bring rays together and diverging lenses bend rays away from each other.

Module 6 — Materials and Performance

Lenses and Images

Q1 Pat is building a **telescope** for her local Astronomy Association. She wants to measure the **power** of the lens she is using.

  a) Complete the ray diagram for Pat's lens. Include and label the **focal point** (F), the **focal plane** (P) and the **focal length** (L).

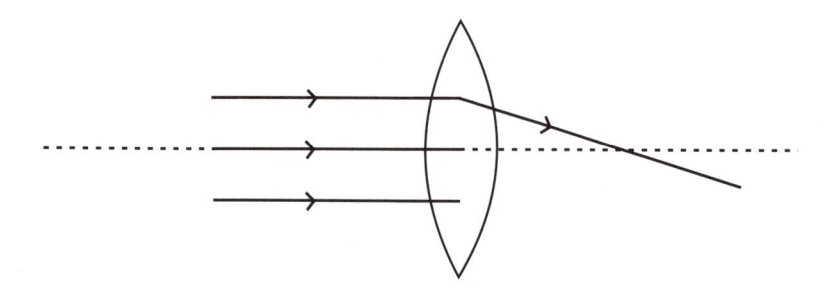

  b) Pat uses the following equation to work out the power of the lens:

  $$\text{Power (D)} = \frac{1}{\text{focal length (m)}}$$

  i) What is the unit for the power of a lens?

  ....

  ii) Pat measures the focal length to be 10 cm (0.1 m). Calculate the power of the lens.

  ....

  c) Pat actually needs a lens with a focal length of 20 cm.
  Will she need a thinner or fatter lens than the one in the diagram? Tick the correct answer.

  Thinner ☐

  Fatter ☐

Q2 A student is investigating the properties of **images** produced using converging lenses.

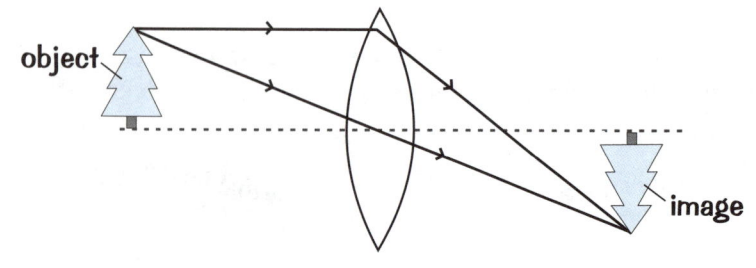

The student produces the image shown above. Describe the image produced.

....

Module 6 — Materials and Performance

Lenses and Images

Q3 A forensic scientist is looking at fingerprints through a **magnifying glass**.

Circle the correct word(s) to complete the following sentence.

> The magnifying glass produces a real / **virtual**, inverted / **upright** image which is the same size / smaller / **larger** than the fingerprint.

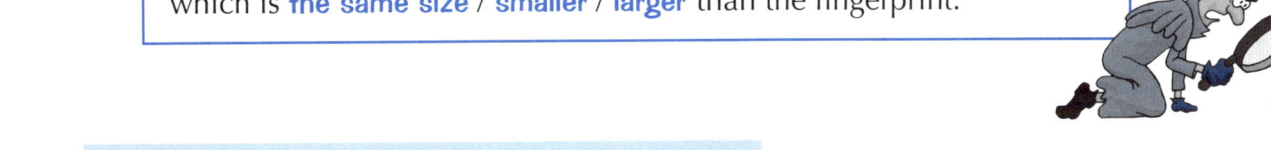

Q4 Jenny is showing her dad some **photographic slides** of her recent holiday, using a **projector** and a **screen**.

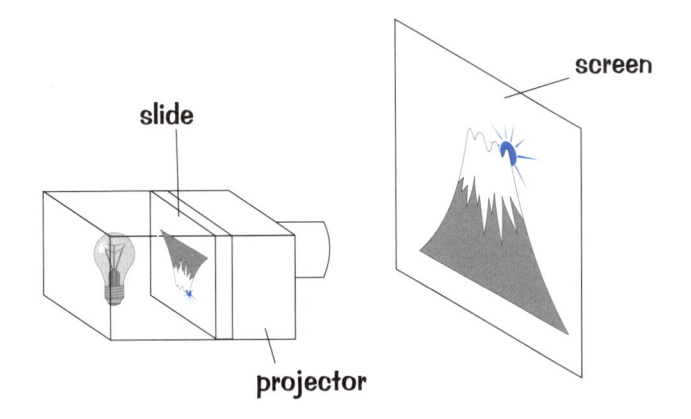

a) Underline all of the words or phrases that apply to the image on the screen.

upright   smaller   virtual   inverted

real   larger than the picture on the slide   same size as the picture on the slide

b) Describe the type of image that is formed at the back of Jenny's dad's eyes when he looks at the pictures on the screen.

....

....

The object he is looking at is on the big screen not the little slide.

Q5 Ellen is a keen **photographer**. She has been to the Arctic to take some pictures of icebergs.

Ellen takes a picture of the iceberg shown below. Draw a sketch of what would appear on Ellen's camera film in the space opposite.

heh heh heh...

Module 6 — Materials and Performance

Camera Lenses

Q1 Mitsuki is a wild flower photographer. She takes pictures using a **film camera**.

　a) Tick any of the boxes that may apply to the images formed on the film in Mitsuki's camera.

- real ☐
- virtual ☐
- inverted ☐
- upright ☐
- smaller than the object ☐
- larger than the object ☐
- same size as the object ☐

　b) Here is a diagram of Mitsuki's camera. Label the diagram using the words provided.

aperture

lens

focal plane

viewfinder

shutter

Q2 Daniel takes photographs of **celebrities**. He uses long-range **lenses** so he can take close-up photos without being seen.

Daniel's lenses have a thin transparent **coating**.
How does the coating improve the performance of the lenses?

....

....

Top Tips: Digital cameras form images in more or less the same way as film cameras. The only difference is that the image is projected onto a light-sensitive grid rather than a strip of film.

Module 6 — Materials and Performance

Matching Properties and Uses

Q1 Adam is designing a new **foil** — a **bendy** sword blade — for his fencing equipment. When the foil touches an opponent's metal breast plate, it should complete an **electric circuit**, making a buzzing sound.

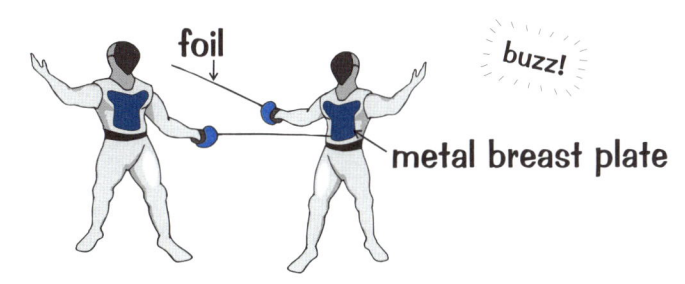

a) From the properties given below, circle those that would be desirable in the foil:

> thermal insulator   light   electrical conductor
>
> rigid   flexible   brittle   strong

b) Tick **one** box to show which class of material would be the most suitable for Adam's foil.

- Metals and alloys ☐
- Polymers ☐
- Ceramics ☐
- Wood and wood products ☐
- Composites ☐

c) Adam decides to make the **handle** of his fencing sword from a composite material. Suggest why each of the following classes of materials would be unsuitable for the handle.

Ceramics ....

Metals ....

Q2 A **materials scientist** is designing the outer casing for a new **kettle**. She has three materials to choose from.

- **Material A** good thermal conductor, high melting point, tough
- **Material B** good thermal conductor, low melting point, flexible
- **Material C** good thermal insulator, high melting point, tough

Which material should the scientist use? Explain why.

....

....

Module 6 — Materials and Performance

Mixed Questions for Module 6

Q1 A designer makes tools for road construction workers. He is testing a new **jackhammer** — a machine used to break up concrete.

    a) Write down **two** physical properties that the hammer part of a jackhammer should have.

        1. ....

        2. ....

    b) The handles of the jackhammer are made from polymers. The hammer head gets very hot but the handles of the jackhammer don't. Why is this? Tick the correct box.

        Polymers are good thermal conductors. Heat can easily pass through them. ☐

        Polymers are poor thermal conductors. Heat can't easily pass through them. ☐

        Polymers are good electrical conductors. Heat can easily pass through them. ☐

Q2 Quentin races **sports cars**. He takes part in the Cumbrian **Grand Prix**, which is 52 laps of a figure-of-eight track.

    a) Quentin drives round the track for two laps at a constant speed but his velocity is constantly changing. Explain why.

        ....

    b) Describe what would happen to Quentin's momentum if he drove **twice** as fast.

        ....

    c) Circle the correct word in each pair to complete the following sentence.

        As Quentin drives around the track the car uses up fuel, causing its total mass to increase / decrease.

        Even though its speed stays constant throughout the race, its momentum will increase / decrease.

    d) Quentin's car has many **safety features** to protect him if he crashes. Name one type of material used in a car safety feature and describe how it is beneficial.

        ....

    e) Quentin uses a decibel meter to measure the noise level from his car's engine. The noise level is enough to cause temporary hearing loss but not enough to cause pain.

        What was the reading on Quentin's decibel meter? Circle the correct answer.

        40 dB   75 dB   120 dB

Module 6 — Materials and Performance

Mixed Questions for Module 6

Q3 Katie is designing a new **camera**. She wants to investigate how the **distance** between the **focused image** and the lens depends on how far the object is from the lens.

She set up the apparatus shown below.

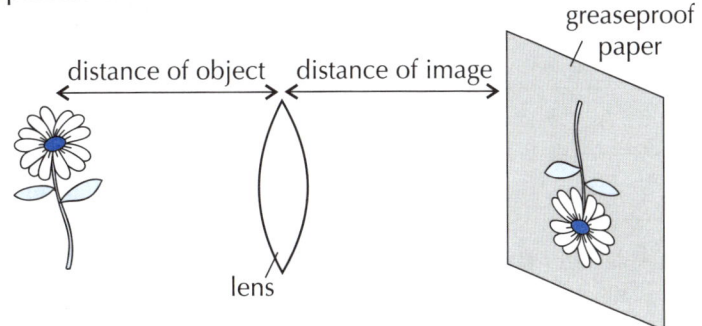

a) Is the lens a converging or diverging lens? ....

b) Give **two** properties of the image formed by the lens.

1. .... 2. ....

c) Circle the correct word(s) to complete the sentence below.

> Lenses are made from **glass** / **copper** because it's
> **opaque** / **transparent** and **brittle** / **can be easily moulded**.

Katie moved the object and then moved the greaseproof paper until the image came into focus. She noted down the distances of the object and the image from the lens.
Her results are shown in the table below.

Object distance (cm)	Image distance (cm)
20.0	20.0
30.0	14.0
40.0	13.0
50.0	12.5
60.0	14.0
70.0	12.0
80.0	12.0

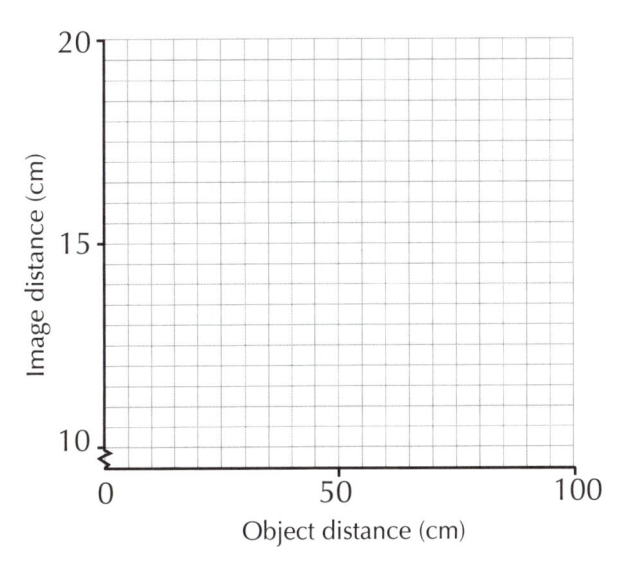

d) On the axes provided, draw a graph to show Katie's results, including a line of best fit.

e) Circle on the graph any outliers in the data.

f) What conclusion could Katie draw from the graph?

....

Module 6 — Materials and Performance

Mixed Questions for Module 6

Q4 Luka was choosing a material for a new **tent**. He had a choice of three materials.

Material	Cost (£ per m²)	Lifespan (years)	Recyclable	Can be dyed
A	1.69	10	Yes	No
B	12.08	25	No	No
C	2.16	2	No	Yes

a) Which materials are best for price, durability and colour choice?
Draw lines to match the property with the best material. A material can be used once or not at all.

price   A

colour choice   B

durability   C

Luka wanted to use Material A. Unfortunately it didn't conform to the right safety standards for tents.

b) Name two practitioners whose job it is to ensure that safety standards are met.

1. ....

2. ....

Q5 CGP Beds make really comfy **beds** that have lots of **springs** inside the mattresses.

a) When someone is lying on a bed, are the springs in the mattress under tension or compression?

....

b) CGP Beds are testing two new types of spring to see which would be better to use in their mattresses. The force-extension graph shows the results.

  i) State whether each spring behaves **elastically** or **plastically** under a force of 3500 N.

  Spring A ....

  Spring B ....

  ii) CGP Beds want to provide a guarantee that their mattresses will keep their shape for loads of up to 4000 N. Which type of spring should they use?

  ....

Module 6 — Materials and Performance